the
Threshold
of
Technocracy

2nd Printing.
This book was written, what I thought to be somewhat
futuristically, just five years ago. This book was
registered in the Library of Congress in 2008.
Sadly, the information contained; can already be seen in
our current events or even recent history . . .

the Threshold of Technocracy

by K. D. Elizabeth Beisinger

Scripture quotations from the King James Version of the
Bible with the Names of G-d and Messiah transliterated
from
the Concise Dictionary of the words in The Hebrew Bible;
with their renderings in the Authorized English Version
Contained in
Strong's Exhaustive Concordance of the Bible
by James Strong, LL.D., S.T.D.

Pictured on the cover, the four horsemen in the painting
by
Victor Vasnetsov, "Four Horsemen of the Apocalypse"

This book is dedicated to our beloved Grandchildren, And to those that will follow

I wanted so much to leave this world a better place than I found it, but Scripture reveals, the changes being made by mankind are not for the better. What I can do is leave to them the Instruction and the example for their journey through this place that is not their final home. I didn't want to leave to their generation the legacy of debt that was left to mine, but if Messiah tarries, the burden on their generation will be even greater.

The choices that this young generation is watching the older ones make, will lead them on only one of two paths, but of course; that has always been the case.

It is becoming increasingly difficult to discern the Truth; as politics has become religious, faith is primarily in the knowledge of humanity, and religion has become self-defined.

And so, Adeline, Sadie and Hayden;
When these things begin to come to pass, then look up, and lift up your heads; for your redemption draweth nigh.

Luke 21: 28

Behold, he cometh with clouds; and every eye shall see him . . .

Revelation 1: 7a

Preface

Saying, I am Alpha and Omega, the first and the last:
and, What thou seest, write in a book . . .
                                    Revelation 1: 11a

Two prefaces have already been written for this book, at this point, as well as three final chapters. Obviously, some rearranging has been going on, in an attempt to achieve some sort of order. I just cannot put into words, the difficulty of organizing the description of what we see around us, much less, the coming chaos. I have asked YHWH to please order these pages, that the warning would be clear. So, here I am writing yet another Preface.

Scripture tells us, and I repeat it through out the book, "there is nothing new under the sun." From Genesis to the Revelation, the endeavors of humanity remain the same. Why, then, when we start a new solution or new crisis, do we act and believe that we are on the brink of something unheard of? G-d's Word says "nothing new." Do I think there were computers in the days of Elijah? No, probably not, but there may have been aliens, at least talk of them! Do I believe there was civilization as we know it, in the days of Abraham? Probably not, but there was obviously a desire to schmooze those in leadership and attain wealth. We see that even in ministry, nearly around the world. Muslim clerics have a great deal of political power in Arab nations, and obviously gaining power in the United States. In Israel, even though it is a democracy that has no specified religion, the rabbis have a great deal of political influence and the same can be said of America. We have AIPAC and the legacy of Rebbe Menachem M. Schneerson who was granted many invitations to the White House through the Reagan and

Bush 41, years.

Modern Christianity claims a foundational part in this nation, and many denominations are quite vocal, politically. Christian chaplains serve in many community endeavors, willingly and often without compensation. Christian clergy have availed themselves in many community services; hospital chaplains, police chaplains, fire chaplains, and chaplains associated with world wide charities. The present administration has even opened the door for religious organizations to apply and receive federal grant funding through what is called the Faith Based and Community Initiative.

America has a 501c3 tax exemption that truly makes it easy for ministries and chaplains to serve for very little. With a 501c3, tax exemption can be granted for earnings through ministry. Tax exemption is beneficial to those who are serving with little compensation and is a bonanza for those that have their families on staff and their personal property dedicated to "the ministry."

The 501c3 is a tricky piece of paper, that I believe, actually quiets the religious voice on the public square. By accepting the tax exemption, a ministry can receive caboodles of donations, but that same ministry is bound to a code of silence or political correctness, when it comes to many matters of national importance.

I received a letter several years ago from the Billy Graham Evangelistic Association explaining the legal and political requirements for tax exempt status. I do not have the tax exemption status of a non-profit ministry. After doing the math with today's prices, I can work pretty hard, speak frequently, write books, and still be a "non-profit" entity, as can so many in today's economy. Once Dr. Graham's organization explained the caution one must use in a tax exempt ministry, I prayed, and was led to the passage in which Y'hshuwah and his disciples paid taxes.

There I found my answer.

I'm grateful for the freedom to be able to choose to pay taxes and forego the required political correctness of tax exemption.

Thanks be to G-d; that for a few tax dollars sent to Uncle Sam, we still have freedom of press, freedom of speech, and freedom of religion; that the warning may be sounded, the prophecy proclaimed, and the Good News published.

Write the things which thou hast seen, and the things which are, and the things which shall be hereafter;
Revelation 1: 19

Table of Contents

Chapter 1

The Wisdom of Man; the Fig Leaf Solution

Before the fig leaf solution came about, the desire to be as gods existed. There has apparently been a longing within creation, to be omnipotent and omniscient. Not only in accomplishment, but even in sin, the attempt to self-exult or self-atone has been rampant throughout the history of the human race.

Our own wisdom to remedy the mess . . .

There is no doubt that the majority of humanity has placed it's faith in it's own accomplishments and inventions, rather than the G-d, Who created us.

G-d even clothed Adam and Eve before they were evicted from Eden. He provided the solution for what the fig leaves could not accomplish. Although the first step of globalism was the exit from the Garden of Eden, much of this book addresses globalism and the last days from the perspective that America may in fact, be leading the way. There are four basic reasons for this perspective.

According to the prophecy contained in Daniel regarding the fourth government, it will not be conquered by another earthly government. The fourth government in the book of Daniel has not been disestablished, but rather, spread and annexed, and of course divided and renamed, thus the iron mixed with clay. America is clearly descended from Rome, militarily, politically, and religiously.

America is still a world super power with less than 10% of the population "needing" 90% of the resources. The American administration has historically offered or declared solutions for the entire world to live by, just as England did and Rome before that.

America bears a striking resemblance to the description of the Harlot of Babylon, in the 17th chapter of the Revelation.

As a matter of fact, according to Scripture, the only way any nation will not be part of the global government of the beast, is if that nation is no longer in existence in the end times.

As humanity continues in apparent oblivion toward the judgment pronounced in Eden, there are two obvious problems with the fig leaf solution.

One, it is a clear attempt to "go around G-d" and His plan, and the other . . . Fig leaf solutions always become the foundation for the next round of problems. So ultimately, the solution causes a new problem or set of problems.

Now that humanity is trusting the wisdom of man, we're on the brink of outsmarting ourselves.

G-d's solution is the answer to man's solutions. He loves us too much, to leave us to rely upon our own solutions.

Ye have wearied YHVH with your words. Yet ye say, Wherein have we wearied him? In that ye say, Every one that doeth evil is good in the sight of YHVH, and He delighteth in them; or where is the G-d of justice?
Malachi 2: 17

He that hath an ear, let him hear what the Spirit saith unto the churches; To him that overcometh will I give to eat of the tree of life, which is in the midst of the paradise of G-d.
Revelation 2: 7

Chapter 2

The Transition

When I finished "While He May Be Found," I thought that would be my last book on the subject of the last days, but I was wrong. YHWH informed me that there would be another book. I've been disrupted and felt terribly unsettled in writing this book, as the headlines everyday lend to yet more details. And the warning that must be sounded will not be popular. I told my daughter one morning in conversation, "I wish the powers of the One World Order, would take just one day off, so I could stop adding chapters and get the book finished." As an author, I'd love to write a best seller. As a servant of YHWH, I pray the warning is heeded by those who have ears to hear.

Establishing an order or outline of "the Threshold of Technocracy" has been incredibly difficult. Organizing a book about chaos has proven to be quite a challenge. There are so many things that are subtle, yet significant to the transformation of our nation, our beliefs, and our individuality, much less then entire world.

It is very unusual now to actually hear about the power of G-d, but we hear about the power of prayer, the power of our military and the power of self actualization.

We are lulled by explanations that tell us nothing. We are soothed by anger and calmed by animosity. We are told that peace is won by war. I heard a country song on the radio in which the refrain stated "Blessed are the peacekeepers," so I did a Google Search and immediately found the "ministry" entitled, Soldier's Internet Church, with Matthew 5:9 absolutely misquoted. Messiah said, "Blessed are the peacemakers, for they shall be called the sons of G-d." We have redefined morality, freedom, G-dliness, and now we're revising the Gospel; and we have been warned of the results.

We now have an anti-capitalist coalition that has declared war against capitalism all in the name of economizing the ecology to "save the planet."

I struggled with this burdensome and difficult task, which at first surprised me, since Y'hshuwah said His yoke would be light and the burden easy. I soon realized the difficulty was not because G-d has cloaked this in mire, mystery and encrypted code, but rather, in realizing the fact that I was comfortable in my understanding, and this book is being published in a country that is comfortable with their popular interpretations. This teaching doesn't exactly tickle the ears of any mainstream religion or beliefs. It has pushed me out of my doctrinal zone of comfort and has brought me to a place of understanding that there is absolutely no hope outside of the Word of G-d, and no compromise with the Word of

8

G-d . . . none!

The Word became flesh and dwelt among us.

John 1: 14.

World events of the last several years surely should have shown us . . . *If in this life only, we have hope in Messiah, we are of all men, most miserable.*

I Corinthians 15: 19.

I've longed for years to write a comparative work between headlines and prophecy, but I certainly wasn't expecting this realization that G-d has revealed.

For whatever reason, there is a concept that "suddenly" the beast of a government will be revealed, rare it's ugly head(s) and with great pomp and circumstance, two lines will form. Some religious groups actually teach of a living beastly creature being the object of trust and worship for the inhabitants of earth. The book of Daniel indicates the term beast is used metaphorically in reference to a government, rather than an individual creature of leadership. The errant concept seems to detail that two lines will form, one for the mark and the other for martyrdom. If only the people talking about the Bible were not so afraid to use the term heresy, these suppositions would not run so rampantly.

Scripture really doesn't indicate the current mainstream teaching, at all. The book of the Revelation clearly indicates the process of the destruction of this world is not as clear and sudden as Creation was in the book of Genesis. The last days will not be created, but rather spiral downward to destruction. The enemy does not create chaos, he destroys order.

Much of mainstream religion teaches that Scripture is not as literal as it is and then chooses to embrace the symbolism as literal. Many advancements and inventions in the past 150 years have changed the course of life, previously known to man for nearly 6000 years. Ecclesiastes tells us "there is nothing new under the sun." So, what about planes, trains, automobiles, modern medicine, nuclear warheads, the space race, and computers?

Technology, although only recent and often futuristic, in it's fundamental form, actually dates back to the Garden of Eden. The desire and 'promise' to exceed the limits and boundaries, at the hand of humanity. Rather than a yearning to know G-d, humanity chose to pursue the endeavor to know what G-d knows, to "be as gods." Eve picked that forbidden fruit based on a longing to know beyond her confines, and the promise to know what G-d does.

This tempting promise is still offered and available, and bringing death today. Whether it is medical procedures, space travel or military might, and many things between, there is a predominant prevailing human desire. The need to know more, to push the limits, obtain the knowledge of the universe, to know what G-d knows, but without seeking Him.

While we're spending our resources, seeking the unknown and watching each other, we are not seeking G-d and missing the obvious. While we fear the decoys and exhaust our youth fighting the imagined or uninvolved, the real danger looms. We will be unprepared to face, unable to resist, and most probably without the discernment to even recognize what the true danger and enemy is.

When I first began the research for "the Threshold of Technocracy," I attempted to distance myself from the information I was reading, like some sort of science fiction novel. Sadly, the information contained in this book is documented accounts, headlines, and legislation of the 20th and 21st Century. In my heart, I've yearned to preserve a futuristic perspective, as in "if we don't take this action . . . This could happen." But it is already happening. Or "in the event of . . ., we may be facing . . ." But consequences are already clearly in view. This is not a potential future on the horizon. This is the reality in which we are living. The fact is, we are living the prophecy of Scripture and this may not be the latter part of the last days. We may only be on the brink of the destruction.

I've struggled with the confusion regarding one world religion and government, until I received the piece of the puzzle that made the understanding fall into place. G-d is not the author of confusion; therefore this unG-dly government will be founded on confusion. I was reversing the religion and the government.
The religion will be the idolatry of self, and the government will be a collection of laws that are supposedly, yet very loosely interpreted to be based upon the Word of G-d. It is this fragmented portion of Scripture, that all three current major religions recognize and claim. Yet even in this collective religious government, this will not be where the "citizens" of this one world government, or new world order, actually place their faith. The faith of the citizens of the new world order will be in technology, everything from global positioning satellites to modern medicine, and it will be maintained by humanity's greatest love; money.

There is already a term for a democratic government that chooses the masters of technology to be it's leaders. The term for this type of government is technocracy. This type of government has already been suggested as a type of democracy in the Middle East, by the present leader of the United States of America.

Technocracy is defined as: 'A form of government in which scientists and technical experts are in control. Technocracy was described as that society in which those who govern, justify themselves by appeal, to technical experts who justify themselves by appeal to scientific forms of knowledge.'

Technology is not necessarily a bad thing. Certainly, I am not saying that technology, in and of itself, is evil. I am not even insinuating that technology cannot be used for good purposes. Technology is a neutral tool. What I am saying, with absolute certainty is, faith that believes G-d is dependant upon technology to care for His people, is exulting humanity and technology over G-d, and that is unequivocally; idolatry. Already, science and technology are presented to have the solution, or are researching the solutions for most all of the problems that plague humanity, including of course, the plagues themselves.

When any of these things or the product or status of them becomes our object of faith, allegiance, or trust, we have erred, and the worship of false gods has begun.

Knowledge and skill are hardly to be disrespected, but . . . Fanaticism isn't exclusive to politics and religion. All belief systems, including sciences, have fundamental extremists.

In the various forms and branches of government, we are shown what we have. In diplomacy we have diplomats, in democracy there are democrats, republics have republicans, aristocracies have aristocrats, plutocracies have plutocrats, monarchies have monarchs, a technocracy has technocrats and technicians; but a monocracy is a government ruled by a tyrannical dictator; also referred to as, despotism.

We, earthly humanity, will actually choose this beastly government and undoubtedly through free elections, choose tyranny. It will be after that point and time that the inevitable eventuality sinks in, and the final ultimatum will be exacted. Remember, Adam and Eve did not physically die the day they ate the forbidden fruit and were evicted from the Garden.

To date, with the exception of Theocratic ancient Israel, there have been no governments established that are not either warring and predatory or necessitous and parasitic, and as these end times unfold, the beastly government will be both.

The threshold of technocracy is only the doorway to despotism . . . which will devolve into a most malevolent monocracy ever established on the face of the earth, described in the book of Daniel and confirmed in the Revelation.

After this I saw in the night visions, and behold a fourth beast, dreadful and terrible, and strong exceedingly; and it had great iron teeth: it devoured and brake in pieces, and stamped the residue with the feet of it: and it was diverse from all the beasts that were before it; and it had ten horns.

Daniel 7: 7

And the ten horns which thou sawest are ten kings, which have received no kingdom as yet; but receive power as kings one hour with the beast. These have one mind, and shall give their power and strength unto the beast. These shall make war with the Lamb, and the Lamb shall overcome them: for he is Lord of lords, and King of kings: and they that are with him are called, and chosen, and faithful.

Revelation 17: 12-14

Chapter 3

Can Anarchy be a Conspiracy?

Many today, are attributing our global instability to a conspiracy theory. The interesting thing about the conspiracy theory is the fact that there is not just one theory. Could the various theories be just a ploy by the true conspirators? As the theories vary, determining just who is perpetrating this cataclysmic conspiracy and the explanation for the purpose, is completely dependant upon one's political perspective.

I would state unequivocally that the prophesied end times, will be brought upon the world, regardless of the political leanings of the powerful, or the earthly power in place at the time. That time is known only by G-d and appointed by Him, not world leaders or world events. World events in the end times have already been prophesied, and those that participate in the fruition are simply doing no more than Pharaoh did in ancient Egypt. They are not actually shaping world events, they are simply stage hands and ushers, setting the appointed stage. The evil events of the last days are not the end, only preliminary to the Second Coming of Messiah.

The majority of humanity will, in the last days, elect to submit, although probably as a group or society; individually and independently to the power of the One World Order. Ultimately, those who believe they have a position of power will merely be servants to the government of the beast, probably with the title of bureaucrat. They will possess nothing more than an elusive emplacement at the cost of their soul, the office of being owned.

Conspiracy theories are abounding, but rather than consider who and how many are involved, I suggest that it only appears to be a conspiracy because so many want the same thing. Genesis 3 tells us the enemy delights in tempting humans to choose to take part in their own destruction and demise. In convincing them their destiny is in their own hands, calling it "empowerment," they self-destruct. People in power, want more power. People controlling money, want more control over more money, and people that live in fear look for things to cause them more fear. People that are motivated by anger, look for something to be angry about. The conspiracy factor in all of this will not actually endure the global anarchy that will precede the apocalypse, as survival will ultimately become "every man for himself."

When we consider the fact that the driving force for humanity is self, there is just no way to organize more than one individual in that "conspiracy." Self centeredness, fear, and greed do not really contribute to the formation of a solid, lasting conspiratorial organization.

The selling of one's soul doesn't necessarily induct one into the membership of a conspiracy. Many individuals with the same goal do not constitute a conspiracy, although they may find themselves attempting to be a collective part of the bigger picture of power. In the negotiations of one's soul, the various goals of individuals may be similar, but each human being has the opportunity to make their own unique deal with the devil. History shows us that most individuals who appear to have sold their souls and made a deal with the devil, did so exclusively for selfish gain, not for the shared benefit of any group or cartel.

As the term global, becomes more enmeshed into our vocabulary and ideology, the drive of self survival will become more evident. Six billion people, all wanting more for themselves, whatever the "more" is; is not a conspiracy, but rather, the brink of self serving anarchy.

The monocracy that will be deceptively orchestrated through the anarchy and ultimately rule the world for a short time, will be directed by the same evil serpent that appeared to Eve in the Garden of Eden. The fact of human selfishness, the interchange of definition between good and evil, and the exultation of human knowledge taking place concurrently, actually appear to be more of a consolidation and coalition of greed, fear, and narcissism, rather than a conspiracy. I John 2:16 refers to these three aforementioned conditions, *as lust of the eyes, lust of the flesh, and the pride of life.*

We are becoming more aware every day of those that cannot be trusted. This distrust factor ranges from people on the street to leaders in power. Social status, economics, or politics have no true bearing when it comes to trust, but those issues do tend to provide the framework. In ideology of us against them, we simply do not trust "them."

The conspiracy theory is truly more of an inverted definition by now. What the majority of people may be discovering to have in common, is not a goal but an apprehension; not a mission, but a resistance, not a coming together or global cooperation, but rather a captivity on the same planet.

The motivation for this [would be] conspiracy theory is nothing more than "want" and opposition. Global greed, a pandemic fear of death, and egotism is the pseudo conspiracy. Everybody just wants, just wants to survive, and just knows they deserve to survive. The opposition factor is simple in the presumption of a conspiracy theory. Anyone that doesn't hold the same views and values is one of "them," leading to the illusion of collusion aimed at the destruction of the proverbial "us." G-d's Word clearly states the enemy is aimed at the destruction of G-d's creation, including man. But the enemy is only one, and he is neither omniscient, nor omnipotent.

John indicated in his epistles that there is really nothing organized or humanly conspiratorial about the happenings of the end times. There are, however; some that have willingly sold their souls and will sell their souls for the phantasy of power, prominence, or provision. Selling one's soul is actually quite an individual matter with only illusion and delusion to be gained, since fear abounds and the trust level is minimal. There isn't enough confidence amidst humanity to accommodate a global conspiracy. There is however a global sense of unity taking shape in regard to victimization, fear, and need. In the event of world crisis, this group will be the farthest removed from any sort of definition of conspiracy. When need, fear, and victimization become rampant, it will not be cooperation that rules, but rather anarchy.

It will be at this time a voice of deceptive reason will offer the delusory solution for survival. The decision to accept or reject this offer will be a matter of complete individuality and everlasting consequence.

This particular pattern of humanity, that many are calling a conspiracy theory, has been recognized and known, for at least two thousand years. Messiah never referred to a Conspiracy Theory in his Sermon on the Mount, but clearly stated a very large portion of the human race would all choose the same wide path.

Enter ye in at the strait gate: for wide is the gate, and broad is the way, that leadeth to destruction, and many there be which go in thereat:
Matthew 7: 13

. . . and all the world wondered after the beast. And they worshipped the dragon which gave power unto the beast: and they worshipped the beast . . .
Revelation 13: 3b, 4a

Chapter 4

Ordained Government

Although Scripture states in Romans 13, the government does have authority and we are to be subjected, or as in the case of Rome, subjects. Allegiance, however; is not subjection and is a word with far greater implication. For any government to actually receive allegiance, the people must have faith in their government. Faith that it will protect and provide for them or fear that their government will punish them. In defining allegiance, faith, loyalty and devotion are words that are used, even being "bound to" a belief or country, which for most; co-mingles religion and nationalism. In many countries throughout the world, there is instilled in the citizenry a sense of religious obligation to be loyal to the nation, thus the government.

As for religion and government, the promise of both, protection and threat of punishment have worked throughout history, and many governments have utilized both methods simultaneously.

Allegiance and being subject are two entirely different concepts that are not defined to be used interchangeably. There are many Scriptural examples of being subject to the authorities of government, as well as the demonstration of allegiance. In subjection to the government, Joseph served and survived prison, Daniel faced the lion's den in without fear, Paul wrote a great deal of the New Testament while serving time in prison, and Y'hshuwah went to the cross. Allegiance, on the other hand, led Pharaoh's army to drown in the Red Sea. The wise men that informed the King of Daniel's praying gave their allegiance all the way to the bottom of the lion's den after Daniel walked out unharmed.

Scripture contains the governmental statutes for a theocracy, but there are none that exist at this time. Many world leaders do fancy themselves to be appointed and ordained by G-d, and since Scripture has recorded that Pharaoh, Nebuchadnezzar, Caesar, Herod and even Pilate were in their position of power by the hand of G-d, I won't argue against the understanding that the hand of G-d has placed current leaders in their positions. With that in mind, however; that always raises another question. Since we know that leaders are ordained of G-d, would that not also include the leaders that we find to be less than deserving of our support and respect? And yet another question, especially in consideration of elected officials . . . Does G-d ordain rulers that the people's hearts desire and behaviors deserve?

I have also pondered the fact that Scripture says G-d ordains the authorities, but often times the individuals campaigning do not share my convictions, so if I cast a vote and my candidate of choice does not win, have I exercised my will against G-d's purpose and plan? I realize there are many Christians that are being told to pray about whom we should elect. I've even heard preachers say we should vote according to Scripture. And to that I would simply inquire as to where elections were held in the Bible.

These questions alone have given me total peace to never vote again. I've been told by several people, rather than not vote, I should pray about whom to vote for. Until I hear the voice of G-d tell me to vote, I don't believe in war, I don't believe in capital punishment, and I don't believe in governmentally sanctioned entitlements. I, therefore; cannot keep my hands clean and vote for someone else to do the dirty work. I'll leave that between them and G-d. Whether we like it or not, whether we admit it or not, a democracy is a product of the Greek prototype and a republic is the continuance of the Roman empire, both of which were hardly G-dly nations.
How is it that the author of Romans came to die in Rome? He was put to death in the very place he appeared to be, according to present mainstream interpretation of his writings; espousing model citizenship.

YHVH has laid it upon my heart that those of us who are alive at the time will hear the words of Romans 13: 1, 2 quoted by the very power that is prophesied in Revelation 13.

Let every soul be subject unto the higher powers. For there is no power but of G-d: the powers that be are ordained of G-d. Whosoever therefore resisteth the power, resisteth the ordinance of G-d: and they that resist shall receive to themselves damnation.
Romans 13: 1, 2

And he exerciseth all the power of the first beast before

him, and causeth the earth and them which dwell
therein to worship the first beast, whose deadly wound
was healed.

Revelation 13: 12

The problem with using Scripture to justify man made governments is the confusion that develops in our faith and dependence between G-d and country. When nationalism replaces worship and governmental provision replaces G-d . . . the government giveth and the government taketh away, and the people call it blessed. Barry Goldwater once said, "Remember that a **government big enough** to give you everything you want is also **big enough** to take away everything you have," and I believe he was quoting or referring to a statement made by Thomas Jefferson.

Eminent domain is the power of a government that is "**big enough**" to take whatever it wants, from whomever it chooses. Big governments do have voracious appetites that must be satisfied to keep them going. All over the world, the citizens are supporting their governments, while the governments promise to take care of and protect it's citizens . . . So the people take care of their government that has grown too large to balance, that cannot support or sustain itself and all the while these same people are trusting that a government that cannot maintain itself will somehow take care of them.

Once the government has fully taken on a "life of it's own," it must be sustained. When the businesses, land, and houses of working individuals can simply be taken to be used for the "greater good," we're already all, but defeated.

Eminent domain is the take over without a shot being fired. It's surrender before a declaration of war. Eminent domain is the death of free enterprise by "friendly fire."

It's interesting in the fact that this nation has hundreds, even thousands of acres being wasted in nothingness and yet when it comes to eminent domain, the choice is always to take real estate property that is already being utilized, productively.

Eminent Domain is aimed at just one group of businessmen, independent business men. Many have suffered the losses of the slumping economy, the greater demands placed by legislation, and will not recover. From the Mom and Pop stores on the corners to family run businesses, American legislative progress has virtually eliminated the independent businessman, yet subsidizes wealthy corporations and maintains the impoverished at a constant state of dependence far below the poverty level. Congressional lawmaking, Supreme Court interpretation, and Executive unaccountability are advancing the power of government and the loss of independent ownership and autonomy.

The interstate highway systems, America's autobahn, bypassed the downtowns in the 50's and urban renewal, all but completed the demise of downtown businesses. The few independent business men that realized their days as independents were numbered, invested in the education of their children to be sustained outside of a family business. Some business people did relocate to the malls or even outer edges of town. As the malls have gone by the wayside, small simulated downtowns have now begun to spring up on the outskirts of town toward the higher end suburbs. Now these independent business men find themselves in the way and the wake of the revenue produced by national chains, in commerce, employment, and expansion.

We are not just losing our businesses and our freedoms, we continue to trust the land and resources to the very entity that stole it from the original inhabitants of this country. Many in America have already subjugated themselves for supply. Although many may argue that natural resources probably should not be exclusively owned as they belong to The Creator, the fact remains, they do not and should not belong to the governments.

Just as we were coming to accept the fact of eminent domain, for the rest of our tax paying lives and the fact that our natural resources will either be depleted or be politically rationed for the rest of our days, a new type of government ownership has come to pass. Fannie Mae and Freddie Mac mortgage companies have given all new meaning to the term, government housing. These corporations are now government run with taxpayer dollars.

Before I continue, let me clarify one thing. America is by far, not the first country to implement this, and certainly is not the only one doing so, now. That is the fact that makes this all the more ominous. If it were only one country that got over extended or too proud of it's pride, that would be one thing, but it isn't. The entire planet is heading for the same arrangements that were made in Pharaoh's Egypt before the days of Moses.

Scripture is italicized, my comments are not.

And when money failed in the land of Egypt, and in the land of Canaan, all the Egyptians came unto Joseph, and said, Give us bread: for why should we die in thy presence? for the money faileth.
I believe we're now calling this, a faltering economy.

And Joseph said, Give your cattle; and I will give you for your cattle, if money fail. And they brought their cattle unto Joseph: and Joseph gave them bread in exchange for horses, and for the flocks, and for the

cattle of the herds, and for the asses: and he fed them
with bread for all their cattle for that year.

NAIS is on the way. The ad council proposing this agenda, doesn't refer to the individual rancher's herds, but rather says this system is for <u>America's herd</u>. *(notice the possessive, singular)

When that year was ended, they came unto him the
second year, and said unto him, We will not hide it from
my lord, how that our money is spent; my lord also hath
our herds of cattle; there is not ought left in the sight of
my lord, but our bodies, and our lands:
Wherefore shall we die before thine eyes, both we and
our land? buy us and our land for bread, and we and
our land will be servants unto Pharaoh: and give us
seed, that we may live, and not die, that the land be not
desolate.

Ask a farmer who tells him what to plant and how much . . . How many farmers have a clear title on their farm? Many farmers now take out loans to buy their seed and repay them at harvest, provided there is a harvest.

And Joseph bought all the land of Egypt for Pharaoh;
for the Egyptians sold every man his field, because the
famine prevailed over them: so the land became
Pharaoh's. And as for the people, he removed them to
cities from one end of the borders of Egypt even to the
other end thereof.

Less than two percent of America lives agriculturally. We are a nation of city dwellers and suburbanites.

Only the land of the priests bought he not; for the
priests had a portion assigned them of Pharaoh, and did
eat their portion which Pharaoh gave them: wherefore
they sold not their lands.

Our nation offers 501c3 tax exemption status.

Then Joseph said unto the people, Behold, I have bought you this day and your land for Pharaoh: lo, here is seed for you, and ye shall sow the land. And it shall come to pass in the increase, that ye shall give the fifth part unto Pharaoh, and four parts shall be your own, for seed of the field, and for your food, and for them of your households, and for food for your little ones. And they said, Thou hast saved our lives: let us find grace in the sight of my lord, and we will be Pharaoh's servants. And Joseph made it a law over the land of Egypt unto this day, that Pharaoh should have the fifth part; except the land of the priests only, which became not Pharaoh's.

Genesis 47: 16 - 26

And we have TAXES, but the withholding for today's wage earner usually exceeds 20%.

For G-d hath put in their hearts to fulfil His will, and to agree, and give their kingdom unto the beast, until the words of G-d shall be fulfilled. Revelation 17: 17

Chapter 5

The Golden Rule

If every major religion has some version of the Golden Rule, why is this world becoming so evil? I realize there are individuals that commit heinous acts against humanity, but I'm addressing religious cultures and society as a whole.

In a world with a population of just more than 6 billion, the organized religions listed here, have a combined membership totaling approximately 4 billion. The numbers of those claiming no religious beliefs, are on the decline. That means, about 2/3 of the world's population espouses the teaching and behavior set forth in the Golden Rule. Only 16% of the world population refers to itself as without religion or atheist, and these people, as a group, do not protest or reject the ethical treatment of other human beings. This leaves only about 10 percent of the entire world with many varying religions that I could not find teaching one way or another. The reality is, however; by sheer percentages alone, the members of these major religions possess most military power and economic wealth, world wide.

Historically, many wars, including America's own Revolutionary War is now claimed to have had religious purpose as one priority, financial freedom, as another, and of course, sovereignty as a nation. Taxation without representation used to be taught to be the reason for the Revolutionary War. With the current tax load; revisionism with religious implication may inspire a spirit of nationalism, but that's only a guess. So often, what humanity may proclaim to believe religiously as individuals is somehow nullified en mass, although we would certainly never say any religion teaches situational ethics.

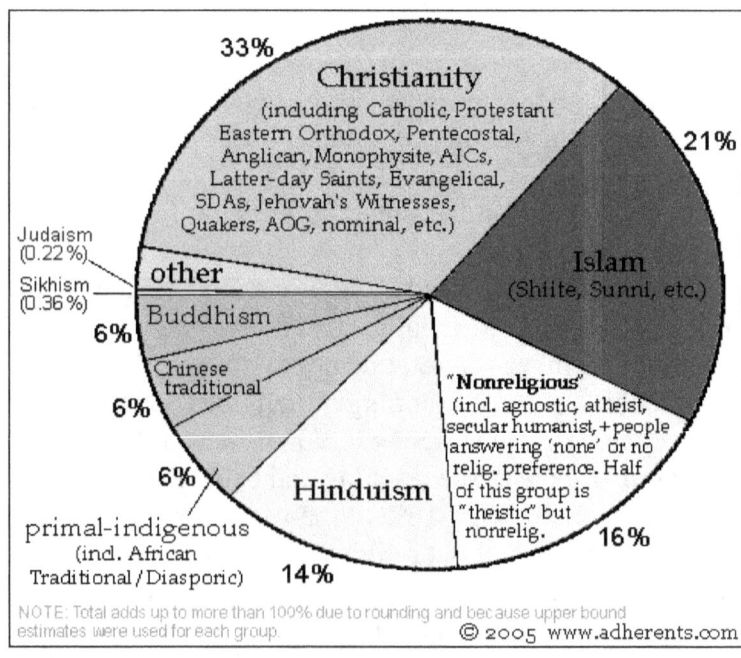

Christianity	*All things whatsoever ye would that men should do to you, do ye so to them; for this is the law and the prophets.* Matthew 7:1
Confucianism	*Do not do to others what you would not like yourself. Then there will be no resentment against you, either in the family or in the state.* Analects 12:2
Buddhism	*Hurt not others in ways that you yourself would find hurtful.* Udana-Varga 5,1
Hinduism	*This is the sum of duty; do naught onto others what you would not have them do unto you.* Mahabharata 5,1517
Islam	*No one of you is a believer until he desires for his brother that which he desires for himself.* Sunnah
Judaism	*What is hateful to you, do not do to your fellowman. This is the entire Law; all the rest is commentary.* Talmud, Shabbat 3id
Taoism	*Regard your neighbor's gain as your gain, and your neighbor's loss as your own loss.* Tai Shang Kan Yin P'ien
Zoroastrianism	*That nature alone is good which refrains from doing to another whatsoever is not good for itself.* Dadisten-I-dinik, 94,5

"The true civilization is where every man gives to every other, every right that he claims for himself"

Robert Ingersoll

Since all of the major world religions and philosophies have some version of The Golden Rule, clearly a variable has been factored out. Y'hshuwah has already noted and distinctly specified the variable that easily rules the heart of man, calling it "mammon." Paul confirmed it later in his letter to Timothy.

There is one more, less benevolent, version of the golden rule that appears to have already superseded the philanthropic sentiment, claimed by these world religions. This will be the rule that will prevail in the One World Order that combines and unites government, religion, and science with commerce, as explained in the thirteenth chapter of the Revelation.

The golden rule that will prevail in the one world order of the last days: "He who has the gold, rules."

The love of money is the root of all evil . . .
I Timothy 6: 10

Chapter 6

The Power that Unites

The traditional class of aristocracy still has some obvious ties to old money, but the old money, serves only to provide entrance into the new class of aristocracy. What was once the elite group of heirs, gave way to degreed individuals, and has now given way to the entrepreneurs of technology and the corporate elite. With subsidies, grants, and loans, everyone has access to a college degree, so the value of such a paper, alone, has declined somewhat, except in regard to the student loan debt. A four year degree has become common place, and a Master's degree is basically a teaching certificate or the door to entering the corporate world at management level. A specialized doctorate is still held in some esteem, but even doctorates and doctors of some kind are in abundance. There is no doubt, letters behind a name open doors and certainly affords some clout, but education is quickly becoming one of the more modest branches of American aristocracy. There is a "class distinction" drawn between colleges, universities, ivy league schools, and technical institutes, but for the most part, the graduates ultimately still become "employees" of some institute of research or higher learning. Although many of these individuals do hold positions of esteem in our society, or are "owned" by grant endowments, the members of this particular class of aristocracy, by education, can be better described and defined as technocrats.

Three generations ago an 8th grade education could get an average man through life, and often an entrepreneur began his journey of success before he completed the 8th grade. Two generations ago, high school and high motivation was the key to success and often a comfortable status of wealth. The generation now entering the work force doesn't dare enter without at least four years of college. There are degreed individuals selling gasoline and beer at the local convenience stores. There are degreed people making more money tending bar than a career in the field of their degree. In the final analysis on the information highway, it is the degree to which one is able to access and achieve through technology and research, and of course their level of loyalty to the powers, that will assign the social positions.

According to Greek history, technocracy, as defined by Hippocrates, was the fall of democracy in that nation. We now have it in no uncertain terms, America isn't even clinging to the concept of being a democracy . . .

There are a few in the 21st century that possess and exhibit the original spirit of American success, which is entrepreneurialism. Entrepreneurialism still provides the status of wealth and aristocracy without old money or a degree. Of course, much of what is known as old money in America is the legacy of early entrepreneurs and inventors of days gone by.

As times and demands have changed and our economy has evolved, much of America's old money is now simply stock on Wall Street, education foundations, and philanthropic causes. The original investors on Wall Street invested in a company that made a product they thought to be of value. Now Wall Street is full of investors, investing in money. In a perpetual economy, upward motion, investment returns, dividends, and the corporate ladder have served to become the backbone of this economy that now lacks a gold or silver standard, or even products, for that matter. True aristocracy, now, belongs to those individuals who live the lifestyle of luxury and do not have to concern themselves with mundane matters such as alarm clocks and the rising cost of living. Their wealth is actually generated by providing the instruments and service required by the various corporations who employ the working class. The working class to which I refer, was formerly known as professionals and the comfortable middle class.

Although I am an advocate of greater and higher learning, I have been delivered from the worship of degrees, titles or income generated by higher education. It did require deliverance for me, because I made education an idol. I truly believed a degree would give me an identity, but G-d already had. I very much felt, for some time, that I could somehow gain acceptance and respect through education, certification, and/or a degree, but regardless of my studies, certification, or title, respect simply didn't come with the piece of paper. I have learned, however; wisdom is a gift from G-d and discernment is not gained by a diploma.

I hope to continue learning until the day I die, but we must also never forget, it was the desire and promise of knowledge that led Eve to the very act that brought death into the world. We would be hard pressed to find an institute of learning that does not offer the knowledge of both good and evil. Can we take the good and leave the bad? All evidence indicates, Eve was hoping to take just the good, without the bad. The serpent made quite an impressive statement to Eve in the garden.

. . . and ye shall be as gods, . . . Genesis 3: 5

Theoretically, I believe humanity has been precisely attempting to pick and choose, throughout history. The problem is, rather than taking the good and leaving the bad, humanity has taken it upon ourselves to redefine good and bad.

The world is in the shape it is in today for one reason and one reason, only. Humanity has opted to make our own choices against the Instruction of G-d. Many blame Adam and Eve, while others choose to totally deny their existence, but there is not a human being on earth that can deny, that the world is in trouble. G-d's Word explains how to treat each other, how to take care of the earth, how to care for animals, how to live in peace, and how to seek Him and to please Him, but . . . We have chosen our own way, time and time again, until the legacy of humanity has become survival and dependence outside of the plan of G-d.

The man that has lead the Forbes Fortune 500 list for several years, is quoted to have stated in an interview, that he doesn't find religion to be very efficient. I found a great many quotes by Bill Gates at the following web address. www.brainyquote.com/quotes/authors/b/bill_gates.html Here is the full quote, I found. "Just in terms of allocation of time resources, religion is not very efficient. There's a lot more I could be doing on a Sunday morning." Some of the other quotes, I read by him, seemed to be somewhat alarming. I don't know the full context of the comments, perhaps they were said in jest, but I do believe there is a frequently a kernel of genuine feeling reflected in wit. He's certainly caught the watchful eye of more than a few religious, "end times" monitors of our day. Bill Gates has said many thought provoking things, and several of his quotes on that page did reflect humor, so I'll not jump to conclusions nor shall I lead others to do so. He is the perfect example, however; of today's entrepreneur. He places a greater value on time than paper in the form money or degrees.

All of humanity has tweaked and tampered with Torah. The Jews have done it with the Talmud, the Christians have used the New Testament, and the Muslims have their Quran. Yet all three religions claim devout rights as descendants of Abraham, to be heirs to a promise. The first 16 chapters of the book of Genesis are what all three religions hold to have in common.

Most mainstream Christians truly believe that Torah is obsolete, or for Jewish observance only, and due to grace is not the standard by which Christians are to live. Creation, the flood, and the account of Abraham remain unquestionable and without argument, a vital foundation of Christian doctrine.

Of course, it is the claim of the Jews that all of Torah was given to them, and as the chosen people, they have chosen the application and interpretation of what they call "oral Torah." Sadly, the Jews have rejected the Messiah's identity based upon traditional teachings.

Interestingly, the Muslims didn't have a recognized religious claim to the Torah, beyond being descendants of Abraham, prior to Mohammad. In his writings to his followers, he included the account of Noah and of course, Abraham and Ishmael. The rest doesn't seem to be revealed to those outside of the reading of the Quran, but it is clear that the argument to rights as heirs of Abraham has yet to be settled, here on earth.

Although Torah does designate certain offenses to be punishable by death, much of Judaism has abandoned that principle. Now, the Christians and the Muslims have no problem with capital punishment, and both religions appear to believe that society in general should follow their religious values, whereas Judaism identifies their religious social values to be exclusively theirs, with the exception of the Chabad movement. Israel, as a sovereign democracy, rather than the Torah observant Theocracy, abolished capital punishment just a few years after it's inception, except in the case of treason or genocide. There has only been one execution carried out in modern Israel, for war crimes relating to the holocaust.

Clearly these three religions will never see eye to eye to share a universal or one world religion, as we now recognize religion, but there are areas of law and faith in which all three religions share a common view. The areas of common ground regarding laws and faith will ultimately serve to unite these three obviously and fundamentally different religions under one government.

I've had so much of this information and yet, the foundational pieces have eluded me. We tend to associate faith with recognized religions and laws with titled governments, but there are some subtle facts that have been overlooked. Religious circles have discussed and speculated for years what a one world religion would be. I know many Christians that are just sure the Muslims will be the world religion and lop off their heads if they don't enter the mosque, but it is an American doctor that has suggested the return to the guillotine. He is the same man that gave to the American justice system, lethal injection back in the late 70's. And you thought part of the Hippocratic oath forbid doctors in taking lives . . .

I read articles inferring that some of Judaism is afraid the Christians will simply repeat their crusades of the past. There are many people that believe the Jews hold a special power with G-d. Many Christians believe, to receive the blessing of G-d, Judaism must be politically accommodated.

In all this fear and discussion of religion, we've missed the point of true faith. True faith is what every individual demonstrates at times of life and death, and the true faith that is shared by Christians, Jews, and Muslims, alike; is faith in our own human advancement, science; primarily in the science of modern medicine. Hospitals, now often called, health campuses are the "universal healing sanctuaries" for nearly all religions.

Make no mistake, even in the midst of news headlines about med students committing acts of terror, good Christians will trust Muslims for health care and a Muslim can confer with a Jew for health care decisions, and the Christian Chaplains will walk through the hospitals and attempt to accommodate anyone's beliefs. I know, I saw it first hand, and I saw it repeated on a daily basis. I sat in a waiting room and listened to many espouse their "faith" in their Muslim doctor. I listened to the religious ladies talk about how Doctor So-and-So, saved them, or a loved one . . . Yet those who truly trust G-d for health, find themselves standing accused and answering to "The Powers," if they do not seek the answers of the universal faith; which is medical science. Of course, there are still those that may continue to exist in this life, beyond what G-d has called for their time appointed to die. Adam and Eve existed on this earth, long after the day they died spiritually, as well.

I awoke one Sunday morning to the religious programming of our local radio station and I was somewhat surprised at the topic, but then I realized this truly was confirmation of the focus of faith. The commentator of this particular religious program was interviewing a doctor for the various health needs and concerns of his listening audience. He asked a question regarding the way the doctor felt when dealing with patients who have obtained health information on the internet. The doctor was very concise in his response. He said when he doesn't have time to go over all the information with his patients, he refers them to www.medlineplus.gov.

Any (.gov) web address is associated with the government. So, this faith in technology and reverence of medical science is not futuristic at all. Already we see that the religious teachers are seeking the counsel and answers of the scientists and doctors, and according to the number of pages and links at the recommended site, doctors are directing searchers to government approved health information. It isn't even a roundabout possibility, any more. Those that are well respected in religious circles are actually teaching that science has the answer and the government will administrate the access of information appropriately.

We wonder what government could possibly arise and be accepted by the entire world. Will it be a tyranny and those in rebellion, simply executed? Ultimately, yes. Will it be anarchy and merely a matter of survival of the strongest or the scariest? Again, ultimately the answer is yes. Is the majority of humanity aware that this One World Government will be a choice of the majority? According to the current lifestyle and conversations, that answer appears to be no. How can that possibly be, knowing ultimately the One World Government will be the prophesied government of the beast? According to Scripture, it is usually only a very small minority that chooses to cling only to the One True G-d. The beastly government will in fact be a choice of many people, therefore they won't think it could possibly be evil. People always believe what they believe is the right thing to believe. That is the precise reason people believe what they do. And few there are, that believe themselves to be evil, or even wrong, for that matter.

The majority will embrace this beastly government for varying reasons, but will, in the end, choose it for the promise of provision, health and safety, and the enforcement of morality. Frighteningly, the fundamentals for this government will be deceptively reassuring and presented to be based upon Scripture. That's right, the enemy will use Scripture, just as he used Scripture to tempt Messiah.

I, personally, use the Hebrew Name Y'hshuwah when referring to Messiah. That Hebrew word literally means G-d is salvation, but in making the point of debating temptation, I've quoted directly from the KJV, and used the name Jesus.

Can you hear the tempting questions, using Scripture? Some have already heard various questions and comments, I know I have . . .

Well, does the Bible not say . . . Jesus talked about going to doctors?

But when Jesus heard that, he said unto them, They that be whole need not a physician, but they that are sick.
Matthew 9: 12

Yes, he mentioned physicians, and it also says . . .

And a woman having an issue of blood twelve years, which had spent all her living upon physicians, neither could be healed of any, Came behind him, and touched the border of his garment:
and immediately her issue of blood stanched . . . And he said unto her, Daughter, be of good comfort: thy faith hath made thee whole; go in peace. Luke 8: 43, 44, 48

It would appear that the issue of physicians is irrelevant if one is made whole.

Does the Bible not say . . .G-d led His people to go to war?

And ye shall compass the city, all ye men of war, and go round about the city once. Thus shalt thou do six days.
Joshua 6: 3

And seven priests shall bear before the ark seven trumpets of rams' horns: and the seventh day ye shall compass the city seven times, and the priests shall blow with the trumpets.
And it shall come to pass, that when they make a long blast with the ram's horn, and when ye hear the sound of the trumpet, all the people shall shout with a great shout; and the wall of the city shall fall down flat, and the people shall ascend up every man straight before him.
Joshua 6: 4, 5

The walls fell.

And the LORD said unto Gideon, By the three hundred men that lapped will I save you, and deliver the Midianites into thine hand: and let all the other people go every man unto his place.
Judges 7: 7

This army had lighted lamps in pitchers and trumpets, they simply broke the pitchers and sounded the trumpets, and G-d took care of the rest. The Bible also specifically gives a timeline saying . . .

and the LORD wrought a great victory that day;
II Samuel 23: 10

And Messiah, who is the Word, said . . .
Then said Jesus unto him, Put up again thy sword into his place: for all they that take the sword shall perish

with the sword.   *Matthew 26: 52*
The same disciple that was willing to inflict bodily harm
in defense of Messiah, was recorded to deny even
knowing Messiah, later that same day.

    And does the Bible not say . . . We are to submit to the
authority of the government?
*Let every soul be subject unto the higher powers. For
there is no power but of G-d: the powers that be are
ordained of G-d. Whosoever therefore resisteth the
power, resisteth the ordinance of G-d: and they that
resist shall receive to themselves damnation.*
                                    Romans 13: 1, 2
And the Bible also states . . .
*And in the latter time of their kingdom, when the
transgressors are come to the full, a king of fierce
countenance, and understanding dark sentences, shall
stand up. And his power shall be mighty, but not by his
own power: and he shall destroy wonderfully, and shall
prosper, and practice, and shall destroy the mighty and
the holy people. And through his policy also he shall
cause craft to prosper in his hand; and he shall magnify
himself in his heart, and by peace shall destroy many:
he shall also stand up against the Prince of princes; but
he shall be broken without hand.*
                                    Daniel 8: 23-25

*And it was given unto him to make war with the saints,
and to overcome them: and power was given him over
all kindreds, and tongues, and nations.
And he causeth all, both small and great, rich and poor,
free and bond, to receive a mark in their right hand, or
in their foreheads:*
                                    Revelation 13: 7, 16

We need to keep in mind that the book of Romans was canonized to be part of Scripture through the effort and empire of Constantine. Subjection is not the same as submission. Messiah was not submissive to the Roman government, but rather subjected Himself to the decision of the Roman government, and in that subjection, He was submissive only to G-d.

Saying with a loud voice, Fear G-d, and give glory to Him; for the hour of His judgment is come: and worship Him that made heaven, and earth, and the sea, and the fountains of waters.

Revelation 14: 7

Chapter 7

Creation Alteration

Remember all the things we, as children, were told at the table? And of course, all of us can remember at least one trauma regarding the doctor's office, if not every trip. At the doctor's office, we were promised candy if we were good. "Good" at the doctor's office meant we were to allow the required invasion and endure necessary pain without exhibiting a voluminous reaction that could be overheard in the waiting room, where the waiting children were being told the same line we had been fed, just before our name had been called.

We were told at the dinner table to clean up our plate, because children in other countries were starving. I never understood how my clean plate helped their situation, but then, I was just a kid. We were told vegetables and fruit were good for us, and they were. Most of us also remember our mothers telling us at one time or another, "not to play in our food." That statement was made for a reason. If you read the headlines, however; you'll find that scientists don't go by that particular rule. Science is now doing everything within it's power to alter the DNA of the food we eat.

One of the most recent examples of "man's solutions" in the news today is genetic modification and genetic engineering. Science is actually being financed and research is being funded, to play in everyone's food! Altering our food, for "the greater good," is just one of the many areas of research and development in the field known as Biotechnology.

Although pesticides and "forced migration" for pollination is altering life as G-d created it, HE has been merciful, but YHWH has allowed us to exact our own judgment in the matter of genetic modification. Scripture forbids man crossing strains, and also states we will reap what we sow. If G-d already said, "No," and put it in writing, just what kind of produce should we expect? Even though humanity has chosen to ignore this command, we will not be able to ignore the results of our actions. Bees are disappearing and dying. People are suffering various food poisonings through vegetation, once known only to occur in meat. Young children are suffering many more maladies with reasons simply not given. Even though genetic engineering is possible we didn't consider the long term potential consequences, nor have we seen the full range of problems that can result.

Addressing symptoms is not the cure, nor is it the Instruction of Adonai. Actually, most people who are placing their faith in some sort of technological solutions are at least acknowledging that the inhabitants of planet earth are in trouble, whereas others are merely passing judgment and expecting an early exit out of the big problems. We can clearly see that famine and plagues are already affecting areas of the global population with the fear of more, looming on the horizon. What seems to elude most of those that are counting on technological advancements to save the population and the planet, is the fact that the "solutions" become part of a new and larger problem. All the while, many are feebly attempting to weave G-d into the technological solution.

I actually have received personal comments from the religious right wing, condescendingly informing me in no uncertain terms that technology is a gift from G-d, while others in that same sector proclaim the pure evil of the internet.

When we are dealing with inorganic matter, I think technology can be a great tool, but once we cross the line to use technology to affect life beyond the recognized limit of days, we just may find ourselves assuming too much. Of course, we know, humanity can argue where the line should be drawn from now until the Second Coming, and we undoubtedly will. I can only say this about what G-d has given, what G-d has allowed, and what G-d intends for our use. It was G-d, Himself that placed the tree of knowledge of good and evil in the middle of the garden, along side the Tree of Life and simply gave humanity, one rule and a choice. The rest is history.

If we truly believe that the Revelation is prophecy yet to be fulfilled, we should consider the four horsemen of the apocalypse, and realize Messiah, Himself has authorized their release. So we must realize, our call is not to fight these things that will come to pass, but rather to continue to teach what Y'hshuwah commanded, and trust in G-d's solution through these last days.

This of course leads us to the next area of religious debate, which is the method and timing of exit and/or endurance in regard to the event known as the Great

Tribulation. Actually, Scripture tells us the Great Tribulation is only one of the signs of the Second Coming, which is actually what we are supposed to be focused on. Most people's lives reflect very strongly that, unless G-d takes them out like Enoch, they are going to do everything in their power and the power of technology and pharmacology to stay. The majority of those talking about how wonderful "heaven" or paradise is, don't appear to really feel the way the Apostle Paul did when he wrote, he would rather be away from the body and home with the LORD.

The fear of plagues and famine is just beginning to be made known. With every proposed problem and potential fear, man has or is working on a technological or medical solution. I believe this is as good a place as any to mention the propagandized bird or avian flu. The fear that is being perpetuated, is that it could mutate. What I found frightening was the fact that influenza vaccines are actually cultured and grown in an egg medium. Isn't that an interesting fact for those fearing bird flu? I'm not a scientist, but injecting viruses that affect humans into chicken eggs to be cultured and incubated, sounds like the perfect way for an influenza virus to mutate. Technology is now searching for new mediums like caterpillar ovaries or fetal tissue . . .

Just one of the many frightening examples of security that is offered, is biotechnology for farming. I found this statement on the homepage of Monsanto.
"Monsanto is an agricultural company. We apply innovation and technology to help farmers around the world be successful, produce healthier foods, better animal feeds and more fiber, while also reducing agriculture's impact on our environment."
". . . A need to reduce agriculture's impact on our environment?" Properly accomplished agriculture is

G-d's plan to maintain the environment and sustain humanity. He specifically stated His intent for man was to tend to the earth agriculturally, and gave clear instructions.

Torah has already stated very specific instructions for the way G-d designed agriculture to positively impact humanity and protect the environment. We depleted the land by not observing G-d's laws in regard to the world He made. G-d's Word very clearly explains to G-d's people, as there is no Jew or Gentile according to Galatians 3:28, how we are to take care of the land so it will produce food to take care of us.

Does Monsanto truly know more about agriculture than the G-d that created this world? Isn't Genesis pretty clear that He created man in His image to tend the garden? How absolutely pompous in our modern presumption. Of course we are programmed and told that we can see that technology is the answer to producing better. Better what? Better than G-d created? GMO is the acronym that specifically refers to genetically modified organisms, which we now call food.

Animals that are herbivores are being fed animal by products. Insects that participate in pollination were not created to process nectar that has been genetically mutated. Most agricultural crops are hybrids and many will not reproduce by their own seed. The weight of most livestock is artificially increased through hormones and medicated feed. Most crops are raised amidst a myriad of chemicals from the fertilizer to the herbicides. Most seeds are treated, and many have actually been altered at the cellular level. One has to go well outside of mainstream supply to find seeds that are not treated and seeds in which the second generation of produce will actually reproduce. The list of obvious pitfalls is lengthy, much less the potential long term consequences of genetic modification.

Upon reading the home page of this major agricultural power, I discovered that their definition of the "perfect field" is basically pre-treated with their products, then their genetically enhanced seeds are planted. These special genetically enhanced seeds are biologically engineered at the DNA level to interact "accordingly" with this same company's herbicides and pesticides for a "greater yield." These very special seeds produced in the laboratory and genetically altered are actually the property of Monsanto.

The farmer is little more than a sharecropper that pays real estate tax. All in the name of "reducing agriculture's impact on our environment?" G-d created the environment before He made agriculture and He created agriculture before He made man. And man cannot create. Man can, however; be creative in his destruction.

Once man decided he could technologically manipulate the life G-d created, he assumed more rights than he was given. With genetic manipulation, engineering, modification, biotechnical alteration, and nanotechnology, it's only a matter of time before G-d literally removes the dirt He made and His Spirit which breathes life.

Most governments with any means at all, are investing in and funding technological research. Our government began providing federal funding in the research and development of agricultural and medical technology, within the last 100 years. As a matter of fact, people lived agriculturally and trusted their health to G-d or at least their spiritual beliefs, for over 5,000 years. I've been amazed when I have traveled to other countries that I found, consistently, when there was a lack of rain, a crop failure, or an apparent infertility issue in either flocks or population, the people sought their gods. Many of these people worshiped false gods, but they, unlike Americans, knew these problems were a reflection of spiritual matters in their lives. Drought, infertility, and famine can only be addressed by spiritual means. Even believers in false religions know that, which truly proves, science and technology is a religion and a god in which many people choose to place their faith.

It has only been in the last century that government got involved with agriculture and began to offer health care. In less than 100 years, our nation's population that makes their living, agriculturally, fell to less than 2% while health costs rose to over 2 trillion dollars.

Technology is viewed to be the answer to agricultural provision as the population continues to increase. Interestingly, the fact that medical technology is prolonging life and prohibiting death in many areas contributes to the continuing increase in the population. Government funding in technological research seems to be the trend, especially when the cycle of cause and effect is so intertwined and lucrative.

As I have said, most governments are funding research and development and America is at the forefront of that endeavor. America invests astronomically in it's government, and huge sums in it's government's funding. I believe it was Mark Twain that said, America has the best government money can buy. That is just as true today, as it was when those words were first uttered. I can't say to what or whom Mr. Twain was referring when he said those words, but my mind always associates his quote with the political lobby, the predominantly powerful, corporate lobby.

The corporate lobby is comprised of America's top sales people. I'd like to elaborate on their value in American politics and the global economy. In attempting to maintain the position of superpower, America must continue to be a world leader in cutting edge technology and research. The place where research, funding, and proposals, regarding agriculture, pharmaceuticals and government all meet is in the D C Lobby. Lobbyists literally appeal and attempt to persuade politicians to affect every aspect of our American culture and as a global power, most other cultures and economies, as well.

Agriculture, pharmaceuticals, and the bureaucracy of the [FDA] all meet in the Lobby. Political lobbyists are the most persuasive, best networked, and strongly financed salesmen in the land. Because of the lucrative returns, one of the main issues that continues to be on the lobby agenda is FDA approval of pharmaceuticals. In addressing this matter, we will see, once again, how technology is truly only a cycle of cause and effect. Monsanto enters the topic of conversation once again, and this time with G.D. Searle Co.

While our nation, once again chooses to fear what some nameless faceless enemy could do to us, we are more than willing to pay to damage ourselves. There is a potential possibility that some enemy could attack one of our cities with nerve gas or some poison. We in America are, in fact, actually willing to pay to be poisoned, providing there is pretty packaging and marketing promises, regardless of the warnings and potential hazard to our nervous system and general health. Although there are many examples of additives and preservatives that are ultimately proven to be health hazards, this next example just brings so many issues and questions to the table.

Aspartame was created in the lab of G.D. Searle, approved by the FDA in the mid 80's after being rejected in the late 70's. In 1985, Mr. Donald Rumsfeld was the CEO of G.D. Searle Co. when Monsanto purchased the company. The timeline and health issues raised are fascinating for those that would care to do even a minimal online research.

One more example of one unproven "solution" causing an entire set of new potential problems. Not only have America's chronic dieters accumulated more syndromes and symptoms, our nation has a greater obesity problem and higher incidents of diabetes than we had 25 years ago, before this technological breakthrough of aspartame. What value has this artificial sweetener truly provided?

There are many examples of preservatives and additives that have been approved by the FDA. Many struggle with potential health issues that are not validated by research standards, but the cost of health care alone gives every indication, the health of the average American has not benefited from preservatives, additives, or artificial sweeteners. I know personally, my symptoms of MS were intensified when I used aspartame, and I've met many chronic dieters with new questionable diagnoses of MS.

When aspartame was first approved and marketed, there was a very clear warning to not cook with the product, as heat would negatively impact the chemical compound found in the artificial sweetener. Methanol has been an issue regarding Aspartame, including the various trademark names under which it is packaged and sold. I found three different references, defining and explaining methanol.

The explanation of methanol from the perspective of promoting Aspartame is as follows.

Methanol is a natural and harmless breakdown product of many commonly consumed foods. The methanol produced during the digestion of aspartame is identical to that which is provided in much larger amounts from many fruits, vegetables and their juices and is part of the normal diet. -- at aspartame.org.

WordWeb usually grants a simple definition, neither pro nor con. WordWeb made this statement when I typed, Methanol: A light volatile flammable poisonous liquid alcohol; used as an antifreeze and solvent and fuel and as a denaturant for ethyl alcohol --- WordWeb

Wikipedia is not necessarily considered by all, to be a source of absolute facts without some editorialized commentary or leaning. I didn't look up any words that could be aligned with the controversy that has surrounded the FDA approval of Aspartame. Monsanto, G.D. Searle & Co. and former CEO, Donald Rumsfeld, were not mentioned in my search or the article pertaining to methanol. Wikipedia simply has a category that addresses the chemistry of Methanol with definition.

Methanol: It is the simplest alcohol, and is a light, volatile, colorless, flammable, poisonous liquid with a distinctive odor that is somewhat milder and sweeter than ethanol (ethyl alcohol). At room temperature it is a polar liquid and is used as an antifreeze, solvent, fuel, and as a denaturant for ethyl alcohol. It is also used for producing biodiesel via transesterification reaction.

We are all predisposed to die of something, and probably endure maladies and discomforts along the way. Don't we know that without millions and millions spent in research? Research continues to tell us most of our health issues can now be linked to genetics. Where do genetically modified organisms that we now use as food fit into this equation?

We usually associate mercury poisoning with ingesting too much fish from a certain area. At one time we were told to not eat too much fish, then we are told that fish is an essential part of our diet, and should be consumed regularly. The "scientific facts" change as we go, but fish is not the only source of mercury added to our lives.

Mercury has been added to dental fillings and used as a preservative in vaccines. Mercury is also contained in the new ecologically efficient light bulbs, set to replace the incandescent bulb.

While I have been writing this particular chapter, we have had the first World Autism Awareness Day. Many parents are quite sure the preservative, thymerisol, found in vaccines is connected to the ever increasing number of autism diagnoses. Of course the CDC (Center for Disease Control and Prevention) and FDA discount their claims, but the Supreme Court did at least acknowledge the possibility in one case. Maybe it isn't the thymerisol in vaccines. Maybe there are just more diagnoses, because there are more FDA approved pharmaceuticals to be sold.

I remember when the research regarding auto-immune diseases was delving into the idea that vaccines may have played a part in stimulating a genetic predisposition to a particular problem. After struggling for several years with the diagnosis of MS, I tried to obtain my vaccination records because I was vaccinated for measles after I had already had them. When I spoke to my mother about the situation, she advised that I shouldn't bother the doctor. Of course, the doctor no longer had my records . . . Where is invasion of privacy when you need it? And so, we boomers have a myriad of interesting ailments and maladies in nearly epidemic proportion, but the doctors and scientists knew everything and we shouldn't bother them.

Although I am sorry the next generation has been inundated with more invasive protection, called vaccines, I am so glad the current generation of young parents is standing up and demanding some answers! I was just in awe of the parents that are questioning the vaccines for their autistic children. When I did a Google search, with autism and vaccines and autism in cases of in vitro fertilization, I could not find any examples of an autistic child that had not received vaccinations. And the statistics of autism in cases of in vitro fertilization were proportionately greater.

When I hear the number of conservative evangelicals that just know the devil is using the education system to get our children, I'm always amazed that they lack the discernment to see the hand of the devil in this strategy of biotechnology and health care, to steal and destroy our children. We willingly follow a doctor's instruction for health, and that of our children . . . Why not heed the instruction and the voice of the One that created us? Scripture refers to children as an heritage from YHWH, not guinea pigs for scientists.

Woe unto them . . . that put bitter for sweet, and sweet for bitter! Woe unto them that are wise in their own eyes, and prudent in their own sight!
Isaiah 5: 20b-21

Prove thy servants, I beseech thee, ten days; and let them give us vegetables (as sown) to eat, and water to drink.
Daniel 1: 12

And I looked, and behold a pale horse: and his name that sat on him was Death, and Hell followed with him. And power was given unto them over the fourth part of the earth, to kill with sword, and with hunger, and with death, and with the beasts of the earth.
Revelation 6: 8

Chapter 8

Choose This Day

Health Campuses, formerly called hospitals, appear to be religiously innocuous in their presentation, their regulation of chaplain protocol, and their universal views. Deceptively, in the name of religious tolerance and respect of all faiths, these universal views deny the power of a healing G-d that shares His glory with no one. When a person is admitted into the hospital, they are asked their religion of choice, if they have one. For years that procedure has been interpreted to mean that hospitals do not interfere with one's beliefs. The reality is, there is no need for a hospital to interfere or openly disrespect someone's religious beliefs. The faith has already been placed in the technology of that institution and the skills of a physician on staff. A signature on the admission form signifies one is affirming their trust to be treated and faith to be restored in the place in which they have come to seek healing. It is easy to see why religions devoid of a healer would be drawn to this solution, but many believe Calvary's Cross is incomplete without Blue Cross.

We have now come to the place in which medical science has become the evil Dr. Frankenstein and most of humanity has placed their unquestioning trust in the hands of these sorcerers and researchers. Humanity has willingly become their guinea pigs, and pay dearly to do so. Although, I consider medical science to be in direct opposition to faith, people are making this choice of their own free will, believing that G-d has ordained and provided this practice. Yet, just as in school and the public square, G-d is hardly welcome. Oh, I know, people pray in hospitals, why there is even a chapel, but the prayer comes after the word and authority of the doctor.

There are many ways in which medical science has overridden faith, and yet continues to deceptively suggest a complimentary combination of religion and medicine, as in G-d using medicine and guiding surgeons. Most hospitals actually have chaplains on staff or in a voluntary capacity and I've noticed, they are not there to share the Good News with those without faith. They are there to offer vain reassurance to those of some sort of self-defined faith. While doctors, nurses, social workers, and those from the billing department are quite specific, the chaplains are exceedingly vague as they offer prayers barely audible above the sound of vital sign monitors and IV dispensers. Since many of these chaplains actually volunteer their time and services, I'm sure they truly do believe they are doing G-d's work . . .

For there shall arise false Christs, and false prophets, and shall show great signs and wonders; insomuch that, if it were possible, they shall deceive the very elect.
Matthew 24: 24

Many offer to acknowledge faith through pharmaceuticals, pills with prayers, sanctimony and surgery, and trust through tests. And since G-d is omniscient and omnipresent while humanity is not, His presence can be called upon, conveniently around the doctor's schedule and visiting hours.

My concern here, lies specifically with the way medical science has invaded G-d's planned command for man to be fruitful and multiply. There are children being made and killed and kept alive outside the divine plan of G-d. For centuries, babies arrived, because babies arrived. Some by desire, many by accident, but they all came along in the usual way, until the doctors got involved.

Now that the stigma of fornication is gone from our society, shotgun weddings are passé, or for the most part, a doomed mockery before they even begin, single parenthood is no longer the social issue it once was. With in vitro fertilization and artificial insemination being the lucrative businesses they are, parenthood of many possibilities now exists. Not only can single women become single moms, our society has carried things even farther with gay rights issues, while science assists and enables. Two "dads" can adopt but they need a woman to start with. Two "moms" can come up with a baby, but somewhere, there's a man involved. And couples without children, can seek fertility experts. I mentioned all of these examples, because they all involve methods outside of
G-d's ordained plan of procreation, which has been working for centuries.

Science has brought about an entire new "way of life." G-d's way worked for over 5, 000 years, and in the last three generations, the invasiveness, power and control by man, has increased exponentially.

In-vitro fertilization flies directly in opposition of the Word of G-d. In-vitro fertilization is done, simply because science can accomplish it. It has nothing to do with G-d's plan for the procreation of humanity. The Psalmist wrote - "in secret did my mother conceive me."

Pregnancy is not an illness. Sonograms are routine with every pregnancy. Why do we need to know the gender of the baby four months before he/she arrives? Aren't you going to keep what you get?
Invasive procedures are nothing more than attempting to take life and death out of the hand of G-d. Albeit, sonograms are not physically invasive, they certainly cross the line of trusting obedience into Eve's thinking; "to know what G-d knows."

What happens to these manufactured babies? What happens to the life that was forced to continue in this world? We don't really know the outcome, yet, because this invasion has happened so recently . . .

In less than forty years of hospital deliveries becoming the norm for American mothers, abortion also became a choice. My father was born at home in 1939. Before his 35th birthday, not only were most babies born in hospitals, abortions were also performed, legally. The involvement of medicine in birth and life has truly resulted in death. I realize many would argue and say the infant mortality rate has been dramatically reduced since doctors began making hospital deliveries. And to that, I would suggest, the abortion statistics also be included in that figure. I am frequently asked if I believe in abortion. I respond with conviction, "I don't believe in doctors!"

Let's address the topic of abortion. It's a touchy passionate topic. I tend to avoid it, because I truly do believe if doctors didn't have god status in our society there would be no abortion. I don't honestly know how the decision can be repealed at this time and if it ever were repealed, I have no idea what would become of all the unwanted children. From the sounds of some conversations I've heard, some would welcome them to the working class to maintain Social Security benefits. That particular notion hardly addresses the childhood of a child that isn't wanted, nor does it offer any idea as to whom would instill the work ethic.

G-d's Word doesn't differentiate between life and choice, but our society does. Although I do not believe that abortion is a viable solution to ending an unwanted pregnancy, I am also shocked at the number of pro-life individuals that actually do not seem to have a zeal for life, but rather; are simply zealous against choice. G-d's Word states in Deut. 30: 19 we are called upon to *"choose life"* and that is for ourselves and our children.

I find it interesting how many times prisoners have complaints about demeaning treatment or conditions and just how many of these incidents or circumstances cited, are very similar to medical procedures or treatments. Demeaning disposable clothing was an argument of detainees, recently in the news. Visit a hospital! Pictures of men in various stages of undress. I literally stood in the gap for someone while nurses attempted to use a camera. The treatments and procedures that people willingly submit to and pay for, would be and should be against the Geneva Convention! Yet parents and spouses that do not want this treatment for their loved ones and have chosen to whole heartedly trust G-d, even unto death; when it happens, have faced horrible, horrible accusations and trials. In many nations, secular science is perceived to be some sort of sorcery or spiritual power. Much of what science offers is revered over G-d or as a god, and this nation is certainly no exception. In our modern society, by using pills rather than bat wings and lizard tails, the mainstream religious have embraced the secular solutions, and believe those living by faith are the aberrant members of society.

There is Scripture that refers to the "miracles" and wonders that would be performed by the power of anti-Christ. How many times in a given week do we hear about medical miracles? And it's just a "wonder" they lived through it? We have been subtly inundated with the notion that G-d uses doctors and His power is displayed through their "wisdom and skill." When it comes to healthcare, the knowledge of 'good and bad' are sought. The equipment that provides this information, the technicians that operate the equipment, and those that interpret the information are revered, and of course are patiently accommodated our time, as we await this knowledge of good or evil. Revere is the root word of reverence.

And said, If thou wilt diligently hearken to the voice of YHVH thy G-d, and wilt do that which is right in HIS sight, and wilt give ear to HIS commandments, and keep all HIS statutes, I will put none of these diseases upon thee, which I have brought upon the Egyptians: for I am YHVH that healeth thee. Exodus 15: 26

He shares His glory with none else.

I am YHVH: that is My name: and My glory will I not give to another. Isaiah 42:8

And

Matthew 10: 8 Heal the sick, cleanse the lepers, raise the dead, cast out devils: freely ye have received, freely give.

When was the last time a doctor or the receptionist behind the glass window, said "No charge, the wisdom and skill are free gifts from G-d! Just freely giving what I've been given . . ."

I'd be a wealthy woman if I had a dollar for every time someone quoted Messiah when talking to the Pharisees, "those that are whole, need not a physician," claiming he was acknowledging the value of physicians! The subject of using Scripture to devalue convictions and dissuade faith is discussed and quoted, previously in the book. Since Messiah made reference to physicians, there were obviously physicians in the society of that day, and yet James, his brother, who lived in that same era, didn't mention anything about G-d using physicians when he addressed the subject of illness in his letter to believers.

Is any sick among you? let him call for the elders of the church; and let them pray over him, anointing him with oil in the name of the Lord: And the prayer of faith shall save the sick, and the Lord shall raise him up;
                                            James 5: 14, 15a

But he was wounded for our transgressions, he was bruised for our iniquities: the chastisement of our peace was upon him; and with his stripes we are healed.
                                            Isaiah 53: 5

And deceiveth them that dwell on the earth by the means of those miracles . . .   *Revelation 13: 14*

63

Chapter 9

The Tower by Nimrod, Today

Nanotechnology is the 21st Century Tower by Nimrod, better known as the Tower of Babel. It amounts to nothing more and certainly nothing less than attempting to achieve god stature and/or status. Genetically modified grains, synthetic blood, artificial organs, and attempting to alter the very spark of life at the cellular level is blatantly seeking to take life into the hands of man, and redefine creation. Life does not belong in the hand of mankind, nor was creation anonymously accidental.

There are many who have chosen to place their faith and finances in this 21st Century Tower of Babel by Nimrod. And let us not forget the similarity to religious views and ideology of the leadership in Babel and later in

Babylon.

According to Genesis 11, Nimrod was building a tower to reach the height of G-d. The stated goal was to achieve the same Sovereignty. The science of Nanotechnology is based upon the concept that man can actually control and manipulate life, from a creator's aspect at the deepest, infinitesimal cellular level. The scientific depth of cellular manipulation is the extreme opposite, yet equal achievement as the height of Nimrod's Tower. The greatest dichotomy in human history is man's extreme attempts and failures to attain sovereignty. While we are seeking to dissect life at the nuclear level, let us not forget, America also has the tallest tower in modern history on the drawing board, slated for Ground Zero.

There are many that espouse and appear to actually believe that G-d, Himself has endowed humanity the "wisdom" to prolong life and/or postpone death. G-d's Word says that G-d considers the wisdom of man, to be foolishness. There is actually a sad reference in I Corinthians 1, that says the cross of Messiah is foolishness to those perishing.

I have stood on more than one occasion, believing and proclaiming that Messiah is the same yesterday, today and forever; therefore He still heals. I can assure you, in no uncertain terms, many consider the ministry to which I am called, to be foolishness. To this day, I've yet to meet, in person, anyone who whole heartedly believes Hebrews 13: 8. I want to be one who does.

Most of humanity is truly looking to humanity for answers. The technologically elite members of humanity continue to make promises and in reality have made some astounding deliveries on many of those promises. Their intelligence, a gift from G-d? Absolutely! The next obvious question would address whether their gift is being used according to G-d's purpose. Undoubtedly, Nimrod was "gifted" in organizing, planning, and architecture. Clearly Nimrod had assembled a crew of gifted masons. Yet, Genesis 11 indicates the use of their gifting was in abject opposition to the purpose and plan of our Creator. G-d shares neither His glory nor His Sovereignty.

When I first began to research the topic of Nanotechnology, I thought I'd find a few attempted projects that sounded like a bad science fiction novel and just mention the warning to avoid the future funding of such disregard of the life G-d created. But no! I discovered an entire world that would basically fit on the head of a pin.

I will give WordWeb's definition of this combining prefix Nano: One billionth $10^{\wedge}(-9)$; $10^{\wedge}(-9) = 1.0 \times 10^{-9}$. In laymen's terms: very, very small.

Nanotechnology is described as "building from the bottom up" but everything I have read and researched sounds more as a plan to "build from the top, down" which seems to me, a lot like starting on the roof to build a house.

Everything I can find in nanotechnology, which is quite limited by my own comprehension level, indicates the hope of building something already in full scale existence, on a molecular level. Please let me qualify this entire chapter by stating I am not a molecular scientist. The extent to which I understand the subject of nanotechnology is more miniscule than nanotechnology itself.

I read an article that explained the conceptual vision of a computer that could literally flow in the blood stream. Nanotechnology seems to be a science of micro-tweaking discovery. There is a nano-ingredient already marketed in consumer products, nano particles silver, which are minute particles of silver. Silver is recognized to have antibacterial properties, therefore it is now present in the fibers used to make socks to control and eliminate foot odor. The results of these particles being "washed out" into the recycled water supply has not yet been determined to be particularly safe to aquatic life. If it isn't safe for the aquatic life, I have no idea what the plan may be to safeguard the recycled water supply for humanity. That is already a frightening concept when we consider traces of previously consumed pharmaceuticals and various other elements present in the water, that are not being tested for, at this time.

Nanotechnology is researching and attempting to develop solutions for problems from foot odor to cancer, and everything in between.

Nanoparticles are contained in some cosmetics and cleaning supplies. I didn't research deeply enough to know if these nanoparticles are of the same substance or not. Used in nearly 500 consumer products and the possibilities of products to contain the presence of nanoparticles are nearly endless.

The research to develop Nanomachines is already underway, as well. Nanomachines are small enough to actually enter cells. This minute machine is being developed with the hope that medical science can at some point, deliver cell killing cancer medication, or prevent individual mutated cells from forming a tumor.

From what I have been able to glean in various scientific journals and research reports, most of the nanotechnology appears to be developed for medical purposes. Although as I have already mentioned, there are general consumer products that have been developed through nanoscience.

This is not science fiction, anymore. I have done a great deal of the research for this chapter on the internet. It's new enough, that it doesn't exist in my encyclopedias.

For those that would doubt the information gathered on the Internet, I would simply interject this thought. I do not believe everything I read anywhere; except the Bible. The internet is not the final word, but if it's posted, that means somewhere the thought to accomplish the endeavor, does in fact exist. Any information can be slanted, overblown, and embellished, but if someone is writing or speaking about it, the concept is clearly beyond just the thinking stage.

Through my search to learn more about nanotechnology, I discovered the research to develop synthetic blood. Although I do not fully comprehend the process or the progress, I have kept abreast of this particular endeavor because of the value G-d has placed upon blood.

I cut and pasted this information from an article at redorbit.com. I was amazed by the date, as it coincided with the day I began this chapter.

>Synthetic Blood International, Inc. (OTCBB:SYBD) today announced that it intends to file a clinical protocol next week with the U.S. Food & Drug Administration (FDA) for its planned Phase II-b clinical trial of Oxycyte® in Traumatic Brain Injury (TBI) patients. Oxycyte is the Company's perfluorocarbon (PFC) therapeutic oxygen carrier and blood substitute. The company plans to submit the Phase II-b protocol the week of April 7, 2008. The decision to file the protocol was made after the FDA accepted without comment the report on the results of the TBI Phase II-a safety study. The company's planned multi-center, double-bind, placebo-controlled study would enroll up to 300 patients. 200 patients will be allowed for enrollment through a recently approved $1.9 million grant from the United States Department of Defense to M. Ross Bullock, M.D., Ph.D., of the University of Miami Miller School of

Medicine, Department of Neurosurgery. Dr. Bullock is the principal investigator for the planned Phase II-b clinical trial. The company plans to do an interim analysis after enrolling 100 patients and then may elect to enroll up to 300.<

Along with the notice to seek approval from the FDA, a bit of information was also given about the company itself.

About Synthetic Blood International: Synthetic Blood International is dedicated to commercializing innovative pharmaceuticals and medical devices in the field of oxygen therapeutics and continuous substrate monitoring. The Company has under development an oxygen therapeutic/blood substitute and a liquid ventilation product, and an implantable glucose sensor.

I found this webpage with a simple Google search of "Synthetic Blood." http://biomed.brown.edu/Courses/BI108/BI108_2005_Gr oups/10/webpages/PFClink.htm

These four headings appeared toward the top center of the page.
1. The Basics
2. Game On: First FDA Approved
3. The Major Players
4. Infinity and Beyond: The Future

The first two headings described quite well, the information contained in the paragraphs beneath the headings. The Major Players were a pharmaceutical company, Synthetic Blood International, a Russian company, more than 2000 patients, and Sanguine. I thought the quote from the CEO and President of Sanguine gave an insightful analysis.

The CEO and President of Sanguine, Dr. Thomas C. Drees, Ph. D., was quoted as saying, "With the results of these animal trials coming in, we find ourselves in a very good position … We have found very large markets, which should have a very direct FDA approval path." Toward the bottom of the page, I gathered this paragraph and heading.

> By the end of 2000, more than 2000 patients had participated in clinical studies of Perftoran, 37% of which involved anemia, hemoraghic and traumatic shock, 19% involved polytrauma and fat embolism, 13% involved ischemic brain edema and transplantation, and 15% involved acute ischemia.<

And what better way to maintain the flow of synthetic blood than synthetic blood vessels?

I pasted a few paragraphs from an article I found in Live Science, because I simply cannot convey the fullness of this development in my layman terms.

Synthetic Blood Vessels Not Such a Stretch
By Robin Lloyd, Special to LiveScience

> The rapidly advancing world of regenerative medicine just got wilder as a team of researchers has reported a better technique for growing starter arteries for people with vascular disease who need replacements.

The synthetic blood vessels could eventually be used in patients undergoing heart surgery to have their hardened or blocked arteries removed and replaced with prosthetics or grafts that would allow the regeneration of a new artery.

Cardiovascular disease is one of the leading causes of death in the United States.

The challenge

In recent years, specialists called tissue engineers have begun to figure out how to help patients grow new tissues and even entire organs to replace ailing and failing parts such as blood vessels, skin, cartilage, bone, stomachs, bladders and even hearts. The process involves seeding specially shaped artificial scaffolds with human cells such

71

that the body eventually grows a functional new body part around the implant.<

To Infinity and Beyond...

This last heading was so dramatic, it literally evoked the thought of eternity when I read it. According to my thesaurus, infinity and eternity are synonyms.
With an Eternal G-d, do we need scientific technology to give us the promise of infinity?
G-d's Word is very specific about life in the blood.

Do we dare embrace this engineered promise? Will that be crossing a line of eternal consequence? Do we know where that line is? Have we already crossed it? Apparently most do not believe we have crossed that line, as we continue to find ourselves being presented with promises from science to address man's problem with life and death. Yet, there are so many Scriptures regarding the plans G-d has for those that place their trust in Him.

As I have prayed regarding the words to include in this book, a fresh perspective of Hebrews 9: 27 came to me. *"It is appointed unto man, once to die and after that the judgment."* I have heard this verse quoted many times and always it has been used to reference two specific topics. One reference is in regard to Enoch and Elijah. This verse is quoted in some religious circles, to confirm that they must return as the witnesses mentioned in the Revelation 11, to be killed, because they didn't die. And the second issue is the argument against reincarnation. This verse is quoted to counter the idea of reincarnation.

Since I have also read of accounts of resurrection in Scripture, I don't necessarily agree with the first topic. Besides Y'hshuwah told the religious group of His day, Elijah had already come, so I'll take Y'hshuwah's word over the interpretation of man, every time.

As far as the argument against reincarnation, I think all of Scripture is clear that reincarnation just doesn't have a role in the universe that G-d created, or in the covenant life that He established with His Word.

The perspective to which I became aware, is that Hebrews 9: 27 states that death is appointed. When I looked the word up in the Greek, the word, appointed, indicated reserved specifically or uniquely; as in a personal appointment. My heart began to ponder a different understanding. What happens when man chooses to miss that appointment? What does G-d do, when man chooses to use "the wisdom of man, which is foolishness to G-d?" Does the judgment begin in this life? I can't help but wonder just what we bargain for, when we desperately cling to and actually prefer promises from the minds and laboratories of man.

How much closer to the spirit that inspired Nimrod's Tower can humanity get, than to attempt to counterfeit and manipulate, what G-d has specifically created in His image, and given Instruction to maintain?

Many of those who are seeking healing and strength through spiritual intervention alone, are seeking outside the parameters of Scripture or if standing on Scripture alone, are being horribly persecuted. Those who are seeking outside the parameters of Scripture, while shunning technology tend to gravitate toward the New Age religions, often in despair of the debates and misinterpretation of G-d's Holy Word. While they have been given the discernment to reject scientific presumption and technological arrogance, they have chosen their own path. For so long we've heard G-d's Word debated, but how often do we earnestly ponder the simple statement recorded by the Apostle Paul early in his letter to the assembly in Corinth.

I Corinthians 4: 20 tells us clearly, *For the kingdom of G-d is not in word, but in power.* Where can the power of the kingdom of G-d be seen in this 21st Century?

Could there be a more compelling reason to persecute and attempt to quiet the true believers? Isn't that about as historically Scriptural, as it gets? Whether the New Age religions pick up new converts, the general population bows down to technology, or the apostles and prophets are ignored; the enemy gains followers in his rebellion against G-d.

Just what is the difference between the tower built by Nimrod to be as high as G-d and our attempt to discover and control the spark of life beneath the cellular level?

That your faith should not stand in the wisdom of men, but in the power of G-d.
I Corinthians. 2: 5

But thou, O Daniel, shut up the words, and seal the book, even to the time of the end: many shall run to and fro, and knowledge shall be increased.
Daniel 12: 4

And the beast was taken, and with him the false prophet that wrought miracles before him, with which he deceived them that had received the mark of the beast, and them that worshipped his image. These both were cast alive into a lake of fire burning with brimstone.
Revelation 19 : 20

Chapter 10

Manufactured Needs for Manufactured Solutions

Which came first, the technological solution or the need? When the technology became available was it a response to a need, or was need then required to be established? I was first introduced to this ideology in the 1942 World Book, when I happened upon (or was led to) the word Technocracy. Following the crash of the Stock Market the massive migration from rural to urban living was well underway by 1933. The technocrats were already addressing the fact that machinery was reducing the need for man hours, while dramatically increasing production. It was shown, at that juncture of our industrialization, that the manufacturing time of one automobile had been reduced from 1300 man hours in

1904, to 90 hours by 1933. According to the 1942 World Book, the industrial revolution was already on the decline before it peaked. With more workers flooding the cities, and the needed manpower hours reduced, what was truly needed was NEED. A market had to be created for the products of this developing, industrialized nation.

Now that our economy is global and most of our purchases are imports, we have amassed an immense amount of surveillance and communication technology and the incitement of fear has served to be the best marketing tool for all these technological advancements. We in America offer a service economy. And the more people that can be convinced of the their need, the more service that can be provided!

Offering services to meet our insatiable consumerism, does not however; lend to a stable economy. It is easy to see by the economic foundation, just how important fear is, in the equation. Our economy is based on perpetual motion and promise of tomorrow's payment, i.e.; credit. If we were still an agricultural society, it would boil down to this. We aren't just counting our chickens before they are hatched, we're selling the eggs before they're laid! Certainly sounds like the defining lifestyle of a harlot, doesn't
it . . . And if these truly are the last days, then could this be the services provided to all those that will mourn the destruction of the Harlot of Babylon?

Although I was not yet in ministry when President Reagan used the reference in a speech, "A Shining City on a Hill," the words in the Revelation describing the Harlot of Babylon immediately came to my mind. I remembered how the Harlot was described, arrayed in majestic colors, decked with shining jewels, and the reference to her sitting in a lofty place, holding gold.

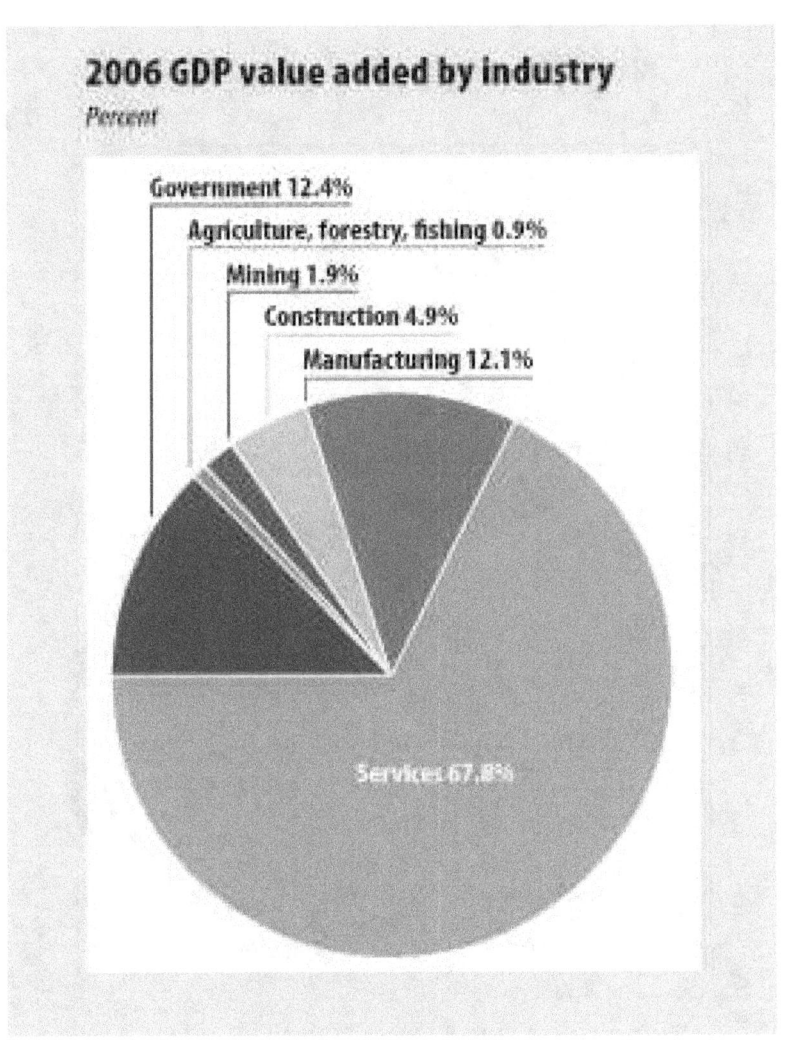

2006 GDP value added by industry

Percent

Government 12.4%

Agriculture, forestry, fishing 0.9%

Mining 1.9%

Construction 4.9%

Manufacturing 12.1%

Services 67.8%

GDP (gross domestic product)

Our imports and exports on a global market

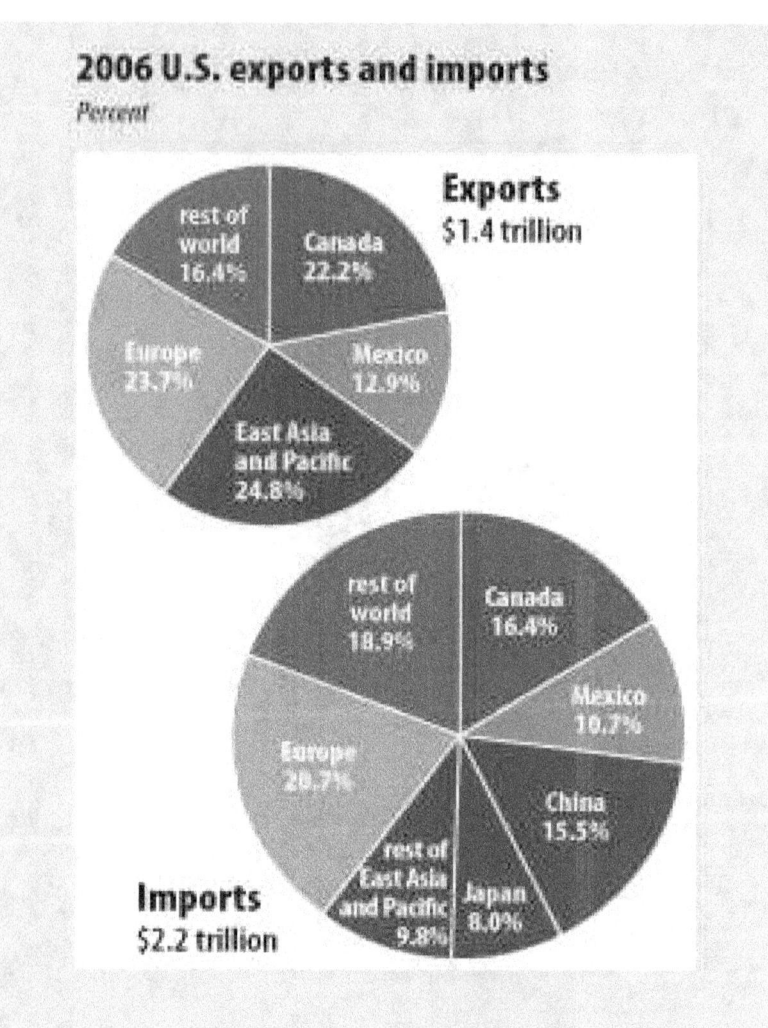

2006 U.S. exports and imports
Percent

Exports
$1.4 trillion

- rest of world 16.4%
- Canada 22.2%
- Mexico 12.9%
- East Asia and Pacific 24.8%
- Europe 23.7%

Imports
$2.2 trillion

- rest of world 18.9%
- Canada 16.4%
- Mexico 10.7%
- China 15.5%
- Japan 8.0%
- rest of East Asia and Pacific 9.8%
- Europe 20.7%

A global economy amounts to little more than all the eggs in one big basket and places it's dependency on the hope that money makes the world go 'round.

This graph doesn't explain what percentage of our national production is exported and what percentage we just keep for our own use. Our imports, however; exceed our exports by nearly 100%. The chart basically specifies just how much of the global economy is dependent upon America's materialism.

As technology keeps going and growing with what appears to be endless expansion, it gives the illusion of infinite and eternal, not only in coverage, but in solutions as well. Solutions become easy to offer, when the need is manipulated and manufactured. For example . . . GPS.

Global Positioning Satellite. Although, the consumers are eating up this opportunity, the fact of the matter is, with GPS in your car and on your cell phone, you are being monitored and tracked. Now, maybe that is for safety at this point and perhaps many people are truly accepting of being monitored. It's happened and now, we can't remember what life was like before the last cell phone call can be traced to a specific tower, or the OnStar associate unlocked the car door, sent AAA, or gave directions to the nearest convenience store.

I've noticed something unsettling, though; with all this. Pay phones have all but disappeared. Technology has taken us to a place of needing technology or being at the mercy of someone sharing theirs. I was with someone in a crisis situation in a hospital and needed to make some phone calls. I looked all over and finally asked where the pay phones were. I was told, there were none, but I could use one of theirs. I said thank you and accepted that offer, but immediately I wondered . . .

What happens where there are no pay phones, all the cell phones are turned off and "they" won't let us use any of theirs?

Which came first, the technological solution or the need?

We are now a nation full of technicians and associates. There are few employees, and according to the headlines, fewer expected in the coming months. Technician is the term for a position of employment that requires some formal training. Associate is now the term for general labor. Technicians are all part of the bigger picture of technology. There are computer techs, auto techs, nursing techs, everyone can be a tech, and the middle class is now being programmed to be known as "the working class."

Remember when engineer was the label of choice? Domestic engineer was a tongue in cheek, term for a housewife and mother, I believe that term is now the acronym, SAHM (stay at home mom), and it's a serious title. This is the segue to the culture in which scientists and engineers are the ruling class. A technocracy requires many, many technicians. The employment of America became service oriented, rather than industrial and producing. In capitalism, service oriented employment renders a technocracy, and customers and clients, become consumers.

Unfortunately, in a technocracy, it is a very short time before the skills and advances of the elite are used to control the people and enhance the system. Ultimately in a technocracy, the representatives, whether appointed or elected use their prominence, position, and authority to further the purpose of the system, rather than the protection and benefit of the people. The citizens all become technicians in some sort of service oriented society and answer to the experts. An expert who is a member of a highly skilled elite group, with political power is a technocrat.

From terrorists to hackers, we need technology for protection, and yet it is technology that has developed the very things we need protection from. We have nuclear weapons and we have nuclear medicine. And the more fear that is promoted, the more protection that is needed. The more fear that is propagandized, the more worry and stress that develops. The more worry and stress that exists, the more prescriptions and procedures that will be required.

Isaiah 6: 10,11 perfectly describes some of the things we in America are experiencing.

Make the hearts of this people fat, and let their ears be stopped, and their eyes shut; for fear that they may see with their eyes, and be hearing with their ears, and their heart may become wise, and they may be turned to ME and made well. Then I said, Lord, how long? And he said in answer, Till the towns are waste and unpeopled, and the houses have no men, and the land becomes completely waste,

Although I do not believe in replacement theology, we certainly have heart trouble, obesity, eye problems, and hearing damage. We have deteriorating downtowns, foreclosures, empty houses, empty acres, and diverted land.

While our government offers technological and financial solutions, such as dream initiatives for cities, medication and health care for everyone, procedures, policies, and protocols to provide government subsidies and assistance, we are not healed and we are not restored.

RFID and NAIS are two of the best examples that I can give, of technology already in existence, needing a reason to be implemented. As an 'organic agriculturalist' involved in small scale animal husbandry, in an effort to live simply, I've been following the complicating developments, but first . . .

The *need* for RFID.

RFID (radio frequency identification) was first introduced in barcodes for inventory purposes in the large chain stores. I believe Wal-Mart was the first I read about and then Lowes, and that was enough for me. Now that the technology is so cheap, I doubt that I could shop anywhere without dealing with RFID, but I do my best to boycott when I am aware. It wasn't long, however; before a more large scale use of RFID was implemented. RFID can register so much more than price and inventory. RFID can store personal data, as well.

In 2006, RFID tags were included in new US passports. Due to possible security issues, the US State Department also implemented BAC (Basic Access Control) in August of 2007, which functions as a PIN (Personal Identification Number) in the form of characters printed on the passport data page. Before a passport's tag can be read, this PIN must be entered into an RFID reader. The BAC also enables the encryption of any communication between the chip and interrogator. With me, so far?

Despite this precaution, the Center for Democracy and Technology has issued warnings that significant security weaknesses that could be used to track U.S. travelers are apparent in the specifications of the card design as outlined by the U.S. Department of State. We have now established the technological cycle of fear, protection, and solution, which with the last solution, of course creates new fear, requiring new protection and yet another solution. Now I ask, in reading this paragraph, does any of the technology mentioned by acronym reference make you feel safe and secure?

The *need* for NAIS, or as I refer to it, the marking of the beasts. We've been hearing for how long, now about BSE (Bovine Spongiform Encephalopathy) and HN51, i.e., mad cow disease and avian flu? We have the technology and the know how to eradicate many livestock diseases, but we also have the technology, now, to control the owners.

I've read the FDA.gov report, and frankly, as with everything in politics these days, it reads like a dramatic comic book. I make the comparison based upon one word used in the report. This writer gave details of covering the first case of BSE in the country in 2003, never mentioning it was the only case of BSE, and here it is nearly 5 years later. They traced the origin of that calf all the way back to it's birth stall before this "much needed" NAIS. But that one isolated case served to destroy businesses, beef trade, and threatens private ownership, still today.

We have still not had an outbreak of the fearful propagandized avian flu, but that doesn't stop the relentless witch hunt and fear-mongering.

Hoof and mouth disease was a serious problem in the 30's in this country and our country came up with an absolutely brilliant solution. America established a lab on an island out of the New York Harbor. In this lab, they analyzed and isolated and succeeded in eradicating hoof and mouth disease from America's mainland. This laboratory has been so meticulously managed that the scientists that work there have specific attire to wear while on duty and change before leaving, etc. Such care is taken that the technicians actually have to take a vacation to take their children to the zoo or circus, so as not to chance any animal contamination. Now, this laboratory that has operated successfully for over half a century is slated to be moved, on the recommendation and by the power of the Department of Homeland Security, and horrifyingly moved to the mainland, with Kansas being one of the potential sites for this hoof and mouth disease laboratory. When we are so concerned over the safety of our beef, why would anyone purposefully take a disease to the heartland of ranch country?

NAIS (National Animal Identification System) won't eradicate or even address disease. It will, however; accomplish a great deal. With this interesting plan, first and foremost the small guy will not be able to afford to be in business with the technology that will be required. Second, every farmer and rancher will be taking care of the animals on his premises, rather than his property. The term premises replaces the word property, in the NAIS registration, thus changing the legal rights by implication, resulting in the farmer or rancher becoming a taxpaying tenant. Only property is protected by the US Constitution, not a premises.

NAIS has become quite divisive for those of us in any type of agricultural endeavor. The federal government, at this time has ruled to keep it voluntary, but . . . grant funding and subsidies are already available for those that voluntarily submit to this system. Although, the marking of the beasts is not officially mandatory on a federal level, there are already states that have implemented legislation prohibiting the buying and selling of livestock without the marking. There are also laws prohibiting the sale of livestock without required certification.

So with one case of BSE 5 years ago, a National Animal ID System has been developed, or the technology was already developed and now this is the reason that we've been given. We have the capability, it's only a matter of inciting fear to mandate the need. Need and problems, problems and need. The perfect interactive cycle for a service based economy and utterly dependant people.

I've only shared a very select few, of the many, many encoded and encrypted labeling and numbering to be able to move about, or buy and sell.

Now I am come to make thee understand what shall befall thy people in the latter days: for yet the vision is for many days. **Daniel 10: 14**

And that no man might buy or sell, save he that had the mark, or the name of the beast, or the number of his name. **Revelation 13: 17**

Chapter 11

Crying in the Wilderness

Technology is not the foundation of evil in the world today, nor is it the answer to the world's problems. The human heart is the problem and has been from the beginning, and it will not be repaired, restored, or rejuvenated, surgically. Although we want to believe man is basically good, that is only the opinion of man when measured by the standard of man. Technology is only the applied abilities of man, therefore neither good nor evil, in and of itself. Frequently, however; in applying abilities, man gets a bit full of himself and begins to entertain the promise that was proposed to Eve. Technology often offers to expand man beyond our ordained limitations.

The internet is the simplest example of technology I can mention here, and not because I understand how it works, but because of the fact it is easily and personally accessible. The internet could conceivably be used nefariously, and is in some cases, but it is also used in many good ways at this point. Point being, the internet contains much available information that can be accessed with just a few letters or the click of a mouse. The information available is both good and evil. The internet may, however; be used by the end time powers that will unite in the New World Order. I say the internet, but there are technological advancements all the time, the internet could be replaced by something even more hi-tech. The internet is a tool, only a tool. The use or refusal to use, and the reason for that decision, is a choice each of us makes.

For now, the internet is serving as a place of information, the information highway, and it is a most blessed place of fellowship and encouragement for those servants that have been called to be a voice in the varying wildernesses. The internet was something that Jeremiah didn't have when dealing with the demagogues of his day. There was virtually no human fellowship for Jeremiah.

Again, I can't speak for the whole world, but it's easy to see what's happening in America as the servants of G-d shout the warning. The god of Convenience has become the cornerstone for the heretical teaching of the convenience of G-d. G-d is omnipresent, but He's not omnipresent to be at the demanding beck and call of humanity. There are so many Bibles in this country, while this teaching remains rampant. We've taken our religious outreach throughout the world, the "godly need for medical technology" and the "godly method of fund raising" and we can't forget the man made concept of "godly government." The entire world wants everything and wants it now. I cannot even imagine the pandemonium that this one world government will profess to resolve, as the last days continue to unfold. Making G-d a convenience has paved the way for the majority of humanity to not even recognize the Creator of the Universe, and certainly paved the way to remain blind to the delusion.

All belief systems have fundamentalists, and they are regularly associated with literalism, although those terms are frequently associated by definition; in the practical application that is often, not the case. Fundamentalists primarily base their extremism on enforcement of interpretation, rather than the literal words of the entire text. Belief systems are not always the religions we've come to recognize. Science has a belief system. Surely economics is a belief system. Philosophy has a belief system. Humanism has a belief system. Even atheists often share a belief system. Although the recognized religions are generally faulted for their fundamental extremism, the belief systems I just named, also have their extremists. Sadly, much of that goes unnoticed.

Beliefs are an interesting thing, and the confirmation of our beliefs can become quite circular in nature, especially when the foundation is based upon tradition and interpretation. It is difficult to actually pinpoint just where circular thinking begins, which may be why we fail to recognize it in our own beliefs. We believe our beliefs are the correct beliefs to have. Whether this is based upon the concept that we believe what we trust to be correct, or because we believe it, it must be correct; the fact of the matter is, people believe their beliefs are correct, regardless of what those beliefs are.

The reality is, we all believe our belief system is fundamentally correct and we disregard, to a degree, other systems or organizations of faith. Spiritual matters are basic, basic to our core values, and regardless of the beliefs of the individual, fundamental to the basic spiritual beliefs of any system, is: other spiritual belief systems are flawed. When an individual claims that all beliefs are

87

equal, then that they are fundamentally universal, also a group not to be dissuaded. Open-minded universalists and agnostics have always been the first to argue, fundamentally, against all specific spiritual beliefs.

The term fundamentalist and extremist has become defined by usage, to apply only to specific religious groups, but there are many secular fundamentalists, as well. Many of the loudest voices against religious fundamentalism are secular fundamentalists.

I'd like to share a couple of situations in which the question asked was so direct, I was taken aback when it occurred. In the first situation, my husband and I were having a conversation with another couple when the subject of religion came up. If I remember correctly, he was Baptist and she was Catholic. She had the generic view of "all roads lead to the same place" and there is only one G-d, just different ways to worship. Her husband was rather quiet on the entire subject although the conversation continued, and I shared my beliefs. It was at that point that she asked me, since I believed religions were so different, did I think mine was the right one . . . To which I gave, an accentuated pause and responded, "Well, yes, I do! I have to believe it's right to believe it!" Aren't we all sure we believe what is right? And if a person believes in nothing in particular, they are absolutely adamant that a spiritual belief makes no difference. I would add at this point, for those who believe "all roads lead to the same place" need to take a look at any atlas or map to realize that is a flawed view.

I am continuously confronted by Christians who truly believe Messiah died to separate Testaments and have no knowledge that by his death the entire world has been invited to know G-d and celebrate His Biblical Holy Days and Feasts. I deal with secular fundamentalists who claim their studies have led them to believe all religions are the same, and challenge me to change their mind.

My husband and I had a specifically odd situation occur, that was just awkward and sad. He had asked me about the date of Feast of Trumpets, and referred to it as Rosh Hashanah. The person who was apparently listening to at least part of our conversation professes to know enough about my beliefs to disagree, interjected their question in the middle of our conversation. "So just when is Ramadan?" I simply said, I didn't know, I wasn't Muslim, I only celebrate Biblical Holidays. I was truly shocked that someone of professed religious affiliation would not know about the Biblical Holidays or know the difference between Biblical Holidays and Muslim observances.

I am not an advocate of studying other religions, but we, most assuredly, need to know what's contained in the Book we say we believe. We need to know enough about what we believe and profess, to know whether or not it's based upon the book we espouse.

I realize it sounds like I am not very supportive of American Christianity, and in it's present condition, I do not support it. I don't agree with the secular scientists, either though. And I absolutely do not even entertain the belief system that embraces both.

I am burdened for the people that refer to themselves as "churched or saved" but the core condition of the various branches of this "organization," itself, does not seem to be based upon Scripture, at all. It's time to open our Bibles and our hearts and hear what the Spirit of the Living G-d is saying.

The Evangelistic Crusades of the 20th Century were the ecumenical outreach that leveled the concept of G-d with technological and financial advancement as blessings for "good people." Through that same time, the literal fundamentalists of the nonreligious and counter religious beliefs gained their foothold of power over the general population, world wide. When the message of salvation without repentance reached a world wide audience, the line between the lifestyle of believers and unbelievers became blurred beyond recognition. This line will not be refined again until the time of the Great Tribulation in which the remnant believers will truly be separate and will be abhorred by the majority, who will of course be self-defined "good people."

We simply must face facts, rather than be lulled by information that merely makes us feel good or encourages us to believe we are good.

All four accounts of the gospel tell of a man that was in one accord with the religious leaders of the day, dutifully protected his government from a potential revolutionary, professed concern for the poor, and knew Messiah, even professed him, publicly. That man was Judas Iscariot.

The prophets prophesy falsely, and the priests bear rule by their means; and my people love to have it so: and what will ye do in the end thereof?   *Jeremiah 5: 31*

And saying, Repent ye: for the kingdom of heaven is at hand.
Matthew 3: 2

And all that dwell upon the earth shall worship him, whose names are not written in the book of life of the Lamb . . .
Revelation 13: 8

Chapter 12

The Pseudo Science of Mind Control
The Foundation for the Thought Police

I know, first hand, of situations in which a select group of pseudo-scientists in more than one country have already attempted to confine true believers under the guise of health and safety. Although, I was absolutely powerless to do anything in this particular situation, except to trust G-d, it was a clear case of persecution in which only one Christian made any attempt whatsoever to intervene on behalf of this individual. When this Christian offered to obtain legal assistance the persecuted believer gratefully declined and said they would have to trust G-d to get them through this and delivered . . . and of course, He did.

When this believer had sought medical assistance, she was at a crossroad in which she was still buying into the teaching that G-d uses doctors. After all, their "wisdom" comes from Him . . . or so we've been told. Wisdom and knowledge are gifts from G-d. According to my Bible, knowledge of good and evil came from disobedience of G-d.

But back to this modern Jeremiah. She found herself in a situation in which she needed physical help to take care of herself for a time. Hospitals appear to be the "logical" option in this country. Or should I say, appeared to be the logical option, as in past tense and repentance. Through the course of this, she became very convicted of the fact that G-d heals and He shares His glory with no one. She has since shared many times having remembered the account of King Asa, in which he chose physicians rather than YHWH. There was no mention of "in conjunction with" or "after prayer and council, he sought . . ." NO, Scripture indicates it is a clear choice, and so she proceeded to repent. G-d told her she was forgiven, but she would have to walk out the natural consequences of her choice. And she walked through a pretty harrowing ordeal in which G-d brought full deliverance, not just for that situation, but from the faith compromise of medical science, and brought discernment, defining the difference between true fellowship and compromise.

She made the "mistake" of sharing with a nurse the fact that she had sinned in coming to this hospital, and she was tactful, she didn't use the term "Sanctuary of Sorcery." She also admitted that she believed if it was a person's time to go, they should trust G-d in that. If it was not their time, then He would raise them up, or His grace would be sufficient. That immediately got this very untrustworthy member of the "medical team" making phone calls.

Funny, this very nurse that had confided her own family problems and dysfunction to this patient through the course of her stay, was now, completely and condescendingly in control. Trusting the nurse was now this repentant believer's second mistake, which she has stated will never happen again. She already knew trusting G-d and trusting medicine was not in any way compatible, and yet, she trusted one of the enemy camp to the peril of her freedom. She should have known better. She does now!

The next person to enter this believer's life was a psychologist, who made an interesting diagnosis when the patient refused to take his tests . . . The official writings, without any testing, read: Grandiose with depression. Let me elaborate here. Grandiose means: Impressive because of unnecessary largeness or grandeur; used to show disapproval. It wasn't long until she had shared this fact with him. The fact that he had come up with this diagnosis without any testing, after less than 10 minutes of conversation, was indicative that the diagnosis could apply to him as well. So, he proved he could make a statement even more grandiose and ordered her confined against her will for observation.

Was this simply a response to her refusal to bow down? My theory would be at least hoping, to ensure or induce the second leg of the diagnosis. Depression: A mental state characterized by a pessimistic sense of inadequacy and a despondent lack of activity. So, according to psychology, recognizing a serious problem and placing great hope in a grand G-d, and not one's self, is depressed grandiosity. If Jeremiah were alive today, I would dare introduce the concept that he would share the same diagnosis. Of course, when a servant of YHWH realizes they have lacked faith or the message is refused, there is a horrible, horrible sadness.

Back to our contemporary servant of YHWH. You may say, that was just an isolated incident, only one psychologist; they all don't feel that way. I can't argue that, which is why I referred to psychology as pseudo-science, as it is not tangibly objective. To the contrary, it is quite subjective, on the basis of the individual passing judgment or "diagnosing." This particular doctor wielded a great deal of power on a very subjective judgment. Isaiah told us "they would call evil good, and good, evil." With the exception of one family member and a Jewish doctor, no one stepped in to help her. Her friends felt "led" to do nothing. Some Christian women even shared that they had prayed G-d would let her die there, to avoid the shame of release into the community, which G-d used to bring to her mind the account of Paul insisting upon a full release in the light of day. Many of her family members concurred with the persecution, and yet her faith remained and grew stronger. She refers often to that time of being more concerned about her faithless disobedience to G-d in going to the hospital than what man could do to her, once she got there.

Well, they could not keep her. Just as Paul did, she requested her day in court and the paperwork and the apologies couldn't come fast enough. The very humorous part of this story, if there is any humor to it at all, would be the audacity of the stupidity.

At the time of her unfounded confinement, she was actually carrying a pager for the police department, one for the woman's crisis shelter and was to be installed as the Fire Chaplain that same day. She sadly remembers to this day, when her fellow chaplains, were informed and how that changed everything for the rest of her association with them. She didn't realize how little hope those in ministry actually have in G-d, until she continued to attempt to serve along side of them.

Those who worked in mental health and social work that she had been professionally associated with, changed when they became aware of her short lived captivity. I can only guess that they felt the shame or realize the sham of their profession, obviously acknowledging with their shunning, there is no help to be found in what they are offering. This profession does, however; grant them good incomes and social status, and a virtually endless list of labels to attach to those confined for job security.

A servant of G-d who believes in G-d's power can be labeled grandiose, and someone that sees the coming tribulation is potentially depressed. The individual who believes these things to be so, can be held against their will. If they use the term persecution to describe it, it can then be labeled, paranoid; as well. That is already happening in America.   There is an entire department already in place in the legal system known as forensics, in which the pseudo science of psychiatry is involved in legal recommendations to the court. These so called professionals carry a great deal of power with the courts, operating on very little insight, making very large decisions regarding the welfare of others.   An even larger number are willing to bow down to those in power for the security of a paycheck.

She has said, it wasn't so difficult to shake the dust from her feet, when G-d moved her on. G-d is greater than the medical profession and she has never so much as considered that compromise again. There are actually people that will not speak to her, because of her faith in this area. Not only does medicine cast a disapproving glare, but there are those in mainstream religion who have openly displayed contempt for her and her refusal to compromise her faith. Of course, there are many that believe someone that claims to hear G-d, is crazy. There are labels for that, too.

I know, first hand, that she told formerly trusted confidantes of the vision she saw when going through this ordeal. She saw two very tall buildings imploding and collapsing, with people running frantically and falling. That was spring of 2001 . . . She tells, under the circumstances, they really did have her just about convinced to be silent. Even though she was delivered and freed things were forever changed, and her peers treated her as such. Could lives have been saved later that year? She still regrets not making more attempts to reach someone who might listen, but she didn't know who else to tell. Who listens to someone that can be labeled? Jeremiah is known as the weeping prophet. He had the exhausting and frustrating task of proclaiming a very unpopular message of warning at the same time the false prophets were telling the people about hope and prosperity and things being 'good.'

In reading 1984 and Brave New World, and I might add, it was back when 1984 was futuristic, I now wonder if I was reading science fiction or prophecy. Since G-d wasn't specifically mentioned, nor Daniel and the Revelation referred to, I couldn't help but wonder why this task of warning had been left to secular writers. Why did the secular writers have to do the work of the prophets? In the early 90's, when I saw the marquee with the movie title ARMEGEDDON, I wondered why we Bible believers had left it up to Hollywood to discuss Armageddon, since Hollywood has never been a true proponent of setting the record straight, so to speak. What has happened to the prophets? I know there are many denominations that teach there are no prophets. Why then would the gift be mentioned and office listed in the New Testament? Has the church treated them as Israel did back in the days of Jeremiah and Ezekiel?

In reading the book of Jeremiah, it is easy to see more than one potential label for him, if he were alive today. As he warned about the Babylonian army, would he now in our society, simply be labeled, paranoid or a combatant? For those who believe Enoch and Elijah will appear before the second coming of Messiah, what would they be facing for the message they would proclaim? Enoch walked with G-d, as in close communion daily. Scripture records many things done and spoken by Elijah. I can only begin to imagine what any reassigned Bible men might face in the 21st Century.

I am not looking for either of those men to return, but rather two contemporaries of the time to voice the unpopular message, and the Revelation already tells us what will be their fate. But what will they go through up until that time? I know what some of G-d's servants are facing already. Although it is still somewhat isolated incidents, the number of occurrences are increasing. It will only intensify as psychology further blends with religion in this "pseudo-science of religious analysis." While Satan's minions are passing the pharmaceuticals, they are charting the results, and those results are being entered into permanent data banks, for the access of many global agencies.

There is a large group of people that actually have determined psychology and Christianity or Judaism to be compatible and complimentary. Realizing that Judaism does not cling to the promises of Messiah, it's easy to see their desired embrace of psychology, psychiatry, and psychotropic drugs, as well as the fact that Freud was Jewish. A true believer of the New Testament has the promise in writing, and many, many deliverances documented in the New Testament, but there is no Scriptural basis for Christian psychology, at all; absolutely none.

It's simply amazing, the number of people who believe a segment of our society is actively attempting to remove G-d from the public square, but lack the discernment to see that true believers are already under surveillance and under attack on an individual and small group level. Frequently these individuals are labeled mentally ill, dissidents, or rabble rousers and the small groups are referred to as brainwashed cults. In some cases that may be the case, but who, according to Scripture is ordained of G-d, to judge? Although the pseudo scientists have the labels ready, it is not paranoia when an individual truly is being trailed or tagged, either by silencing through counseling, captivity by order of the court, or chemical fetters known as psychotropic pharmaceuticals.

Whether it was more than one occasion or simply noted in more that one account of the Gospel, Y'hshuwah was "diagnosed" with a mental health label, rather to say, misdiagnosed. Mark 3: 21 tells us, even his friends joined the judgment of the day. "And when his friends heard of it, they went out to lay hold on him: for they said, He is beside himself."

John 10:20 gives a clear indication of just how much credibility one has, socially, once a label has been used. "And many of them said, He hath a devil, and is mad; why hear ye him?"

The two belief systems do not work in tandem or in a complimentary way. Y'hshuwah offered deliverance, as did his disciples, and the Word of G-d is living. If a person had a G-d given burden and call to help those with mental health issues, they would not seek the world's methods, or enforce them. G-d's servants must still have faith that deliverance or healing is possible by G-d. They

98

would trust G-d to help the lost, confused souls, and not silence the servants, and have the discernment to know the difference; and they would be absolutely diligent to glorify G-d in their work. Their personal lives would reflect the logical, not worldly, balance of mental health.

As far as focusing on the past for answers and insight . . . We have the Scriptural account of Lot's wife.

With regard to choosing pharmaceuticals over deliverance, Scripture is absolutely clear in forbidding G-d's people to seek a sorcerer. Psychology and Psychiatry are only specified branches of a philosophy that deifies the professionals and affords those seeking help, enablement, and those that refuse to revere this powerful philosophy, a label and indefinite captivity. The pseudo-science that exults itself to address mental health is nothing more than the powerful undermining against G-d's promise to believers: "the mind of Messiah."

Joy Behar, of The View, made what I found to be a headlining statement. She said psychotropic medications had removed saints or prophets from the planet. No one was hearing voices any more. Apparently, much of the American religious would concur with this irreverent comedienne.

Old Testament Scriptures clearly indicate that many of G-d's prophets did not think like the general society of the day. There is no New Testament Scripture that even remotely indicates two opposing belief systems could be complimentary. Ultimately, the mental health initiatives, with psychotropic pharmaceuticals, will be one of the tools used to silence the voice of G-d's prophets. We can read now, about people being shot and/or killed for not taking their medications properly and inappropriate vocalization in US airports and on public streets . . . Of course we are also told, it is for safety reasons and we accept it because it's done by law enforcement. If only more of the earth's inhabitants had eyes to see. There are many "good religious people" that devoutly believe in this ungodly power they serve.

Having served as a community chaplain in the State Psychiatric Hospital for 10 years to take Bible Studies into the various wards, I truly must say, I have nothing but strong words against this demonic practice. Society has embraced the chemical fettering of those who are different and these institutions will undoubtedly be the modern cisterns and empty wells endured by G-d's servants in Scripture. This power is already stealing the children. I've had it, unashamedly, explained to me just how the parent's are deceived into relinquishing their children. I've also seen those same children, sometimes years later, walking the streets, released no better than when their parents took them for help, and lost them.

I clearly remember walking past those guards and nurses and knowing, just like Obadiah, I was taking bread and water to a few prophets in caves and to those in captivity that were offered no hope of G-d, simply the hopelessness of sorcery, pharmaceuticals, and interminable captivity. The only choice those people were allowed was whether or not to attend the Bible Study. The ones who realized I was there without being paid or part of the system were the ones that embraced the message I brought.

The part that challenges me, is to have compassion for the professionals that hold these captives. I was still serving as chaplain as I watched mandatory mental health care and the prison system begin to merge.

But he that is spiritual judgeth all things, yet he himself is judged of no man. For who hath known the mind of

the Lord, that he may instruct him? But we have the
mind of Messiah.

I Corinthians 2: 15, 16

Neither have we obeyed the voice of YHWH our G-d, to
walk in his laws, which he set before us by His servants
the prophets.

Daniel 9: 10

And the light of a candle shall shine no more at all in
thee; and the voice of the bridegroom and of the bride
shall be heard no more at all in thee: for thy merchants
were the great men of the earth; for by thy sorceries
were all nations deceived.

Revelation 18: 23

Chapter 13

VIPs

The former colloquial term for VIPs was Doctors, Lawyers, and Indian Chiefs, as they have been the revered members of society since records have been kept. Scripture tells of an account two thousand years ago in which a woman gave physicians all she had, in a failed attempt to be healed. The term lawyer has evolved. What was once the term for those that could explain the law, has become the title of those that know best how to persuade regarding the law. And for the most part, Indian Chiefs have become the symbolic embodiment of the loss of freedoms.

There are no heads of states or national leaders that I am aware of that do not seek advice and take direction from their physician, seek the blessing of some minister, and of course retain advisors and legal protection.

Every culture has had their revered medicine men and elders. Even if we fail to acknowledge the existence, and refuse to use the terms in varying cultures, all government, each religion, and every branch of science has it's hierarchy of aristocracy, gerontocracy, and plutocracy.

The aristocrats are the elite simply by recognition. It may be by name, field of expertise, tenure, wealth, a variety of things, but aristocrats are the lofty members of a society, an organization, or a culture. In every group of people there is an aristocrat.

The term gerontocracy is simply a reference to old men being in authority. Which is an interesting fact of life, one way or another, but it truly depends upon which side of the issue one finds oneself. The inflection is pure perspective and semantics. If the authority of the "old timer authority" is on your side, then gerontocracy is defined as respecting elders and a value of tradition. If the "old timer authority" is not on your side, it's cronyism.

Plutocracy is simply a political system in which the ruling power belongs to the wealthy. World history certainly has demonstrated that money and prevailing power go hand in hand. America's current events, unfortunately; are no indication that we have learned anything from history.

The science of technology has only served to enhance these aforementioned groups and set them even further above the mere ignorant mortals. Just the term doctor opens doors and grants status in many nations, regardless of the field of the degree or ability of the individual. In all fairness to some very devoted individuals of history, I make pretty strong statements about the medical profession, but there are exceptions in the field of health care. Physicians were not always pharmaceutical salesmen. Some actually began as apothecaries, blending herbs for ointments, salves, and anointing oils. Even in the last century there were osteopaths that did not write prescriptions and clearly attempted to nourish the human body back to health.

There are still some chiropractors that actually maintain that proper alignment and nutrition are what the body needs and that's all the body needs . . . But, as in all areas of specialty, there are those that simply enjoy the title of Dr. I have been privileged to know and work with some outstanding chiropractors who truly live according to their teaching. I've witnessed fevers break and respiratory ailments improve, many back and neck problems alleviated, as a result of chiropractic adjustment and without the technical gadgetry of the new generation practitioners.

Many things have started with quite honorable intentions and then along the way, magic and sorcery, then pharmacy, technology, and money removed G-d from the healing equation. Actually, the magic and sorcery practiced by the ancient spiritual medicine men had a spiritual basis, although their beliefs were not based upon the G-d of Scripture, their methods at least acknowledged that physical health related to someone's spiritual state. The G-d of Scripture stated it very clearly in Exodus 15:26. *And said, If thou wilt diligently hearken to the voice of YHWH thy G-d, and wilt do that which is right in his sight, and wilt give ear to his commandments, and keep all his statutes, I will put none of these diseases upon thee, which I have brought upon the Egyptians: for I am YHWH that healeth thee.*

The other reality concerning the title of Dr. which can belong to anyone in any area of education, is the increased number of those that have obtained this status of highly skilled scientists and engineers. The title of doctor is considered to be a position of authority around the world. Promoting education is one of the foundational cornerstones upon which technocracy is built.

Doctors, Lawyers and Indian Chiefs have become the

Politicians, Pundits and Preachers, with even the propensity to overlap, with the exception of the Indian Chief. The Indian Chief lost power in his attempt to compromise. Doctors have become politicians and tort reform was the transfer of power from the people to the technocrats.

The craft of word-smithing and persuasion has moved from Lawyers to the pundits, and the term wordsmith has been all but removed from the English-American lexicon. When a man speaks in authority on news items, yet claims to be an entertainer, any person who is aware of those facts and continues to believe they are being informed, is simply choosing to be ignorant or confused or both.

Preachers have replaced the traditionally recognized spiritual leaders dating back to Biblical times. Indian Chiefs, although practicing their religion differently, were similar in community stature to the High Priests of Israel, in that they were spiritual leaders as well as the authority concerning direction of the people and physical health. The term preacher is rarely used as it was in Scripture any more. Usually we hear the word pastor, and with it comes authority, not necessarily from G-d but more in direct proportion to the size of their particular congregation.

Nurse is another Scriptural term that has been redefined in our modern society. A nurse was a position designated clearly in Scripture, as was midwife. Scripturally, nurses answered to the family and it appears to be a life call, so to speak. Rebekah's nurse stayed with her throughout her lifetime. This indicates the vocation of nurse appeared to be a matter of service in which a woman lived with her "charge." Being a nurse to that individual was her designated life's work, as well as her life.

At some point, the term nurse changed from a woman dedicating her life to G-d or a particular family; to a well paid professional career, in which these professionals now answer to physicians, and the system, rather than G-d. Y'hshuah said we could not serve two masters. Using Scriptural titles with positions that have changed by cultural usage, is confusion.

Now that our health system has run with the concept and practice of Nurse Practitioners, doctors are becoming the great unseen power in our technological dependence. Nurses are the representatives to the awaiting masses that will be required to prove their need for being granted audience with the doctor, or simply programmed to be satisfied to be seen by the representative.

Few people have anything good to say about a lawyer. But few people, there are today, that have not used the services of one to resolve issues G-d has said He will tend to. Scripture tells us, the spirit of G-d will give us the words to say when we are brought before magistrates.

Preachers have become the mediators between many people and their belief in G-d. Scripture tells us there is one mediator, and he is a man, but he is the Messiah. If only senior pastors of the mega Church could see the historic cost of compromise made by the Indian Chief. Or perhaps they have and now choose a bit of inaccessibility to maintain their authority.

It seems we have become accustomed and accepting of doctors, lawyers, and mega church pastors operating much in the same way as the Wizard of Oz, barely accessible and authoritatively untouchable.

Fortunately, the remnant does not have to settle for this cultural paradigm of the New Word Order. Mind you, the truth is not and will not be popular, but the promise is beyond compare.

For we have not an high priest which cannot be

touched . . .
Hebrews 4: 15

And there was given him dominion, and glory, and a kingdom, that all people, nations, and languages, should serve him: his dominion is an everlasting dominion, which shall not pass away, and his kingdom that which shall not be destroyed.
Daniel 7: 14

And the city had no need of the sun, neither of the moon, to shine in it: for the glory of G-d did lighten it, and the Lamb is the light thereof . . . And there shall in no wise enter into it any thing that defileth, neither whatsoever worketh abomination, or maketh a lie: but they which are written in the Lamb's book of life.
Revelation 21: 23, 27

Chapter 14

Deception, Disaster, and Decoys

. . . The Ties that Bind

Defining diligent patriotism and defiant dissidence are the decoys that will distract the majority from recognizing the dragon that will dominate the world in the last days. Those of us that truly love freedom and the independence once enjoyed in this nation by the original inhabitants, discovered by the early settlers are now the exception and minority, rather than the national rule. For the most part, the citizens of this nation do not want independence and they do not want freedom and they either fear, abhor, or simply discount those who do. Many who believe themselves to be patriots appear to actually prefer to just be patronized.

Most people have now realized safety and freedom are not enjoyed in tandem, but rather a choice to be made or mandated. The majority of our populace seems to prefer safety, or at least went along with that premise, and are now becoming aware of the loss of freedom. The problem with freedom is, it's elusive presence and definition. Freedom, simply cannot be kept in a ballot box or locked away for safe keeping. Once it's been exchanged, lost, or given up, it's very difficult to ever regain, and even more difficult to pinpoint the place and time of it's loss. Isn't it interesting that the leader of the "free world" is not free to publicly state his beliefs? Or so say the faithful followers. Why, can we not see the flaw in this thinking? Just how free are we?

Scripture tells us, *"He who the Son sets free is free indeed . . ."* How can freedom forbid the mention of his Name?

For generations, each tried to give to the next one the best of what they hoped for or the core of what they valued, but . . . values gave way to materialism and greed. This nation lost the values of Abraham some years back. Abraham knew his wealth was a blessing from G-d, and to be shared. He asked G-d of what value were all of his assets if he had no heir? We certainly are not going to hear much of that perspective in the 21st Century.

Every generation should give the next generation what they truly value, but that's been the exception rather than the rule since the Great Depression in America. Or maybe not. Perhaps the Great Depression was the defining point for values based upon materialism, which has certainly gained momentum, since that time. I know I wanted to instill in my daughter a true sense of independence and a love of freedom, but she's since indicated, she'd have preferred some materialism. She, like so many young mothers, goes to work every day, believing that to be the best way to provide for her children, because it now takes two incomes to just survive. At least it requires two incomes to live at the level and standard our society tells us we should desire.

She's not as "individualistic" as her mother, but her life in many ways reflects independence and I believe she values freedom! Even though her thinking is much more centered toward mainstream, I'm of course glad to see that she has received at least in part what I hoped to give her. In the true spirit of freedom, I as a parent, have to remember a child should have the freedom to be different than their parents. She's an intelligent woman, she knows she will never acquire and amass the material fortunes of previous generations. It is simply no longer possible. The American materialism of the 20th Century will not endure the lifetime of the baby boomer generation, much less the next. She speaks of how her generation has accepted the fact of that fate. She is, however; counting on her dissident mother to keep her posted regarding the true impending destruction, rather than the pervasive dread of terror and bombastic promises that have caused the definitions of fear and faith to be transposed.

We live in a time that has never before existed. Even though there is nothing new under the sun and people are still people, the world has never been so full. This planet is filled with inhabitants that all interact to have more and be more, as the available space and resources continue to dwindle. I'm amazed at the number of people, my age and older, as I speak of the younger generation and what they will face. The responses I hear, I find truly calloused and selfish. "These young people will just have to learn to manage better." "These young people will need to tighten their belts in other areas." "They will just have to prioritize."

"These young people have been given everything . . ."
And these young people are having more taxes withheld than any previous generation.

The bottom line is a frightening fact. I can't speak for all nations, but the headlines seem to indicate the attitude may be globally pandemic. There is a true mentality of being owed, and there is only one letter difference between OWED and OWNED. The mentality of entitlement from cradle to grave will be a motivating factor in receiving the mark of the beast.

Although this next point could have been included in the following chapter, I didn't include it in the "Blame Game" because I felt it needed to actually be addressed mathematically, rather than simply listed.

I have been alive for 50 years, now, and in that time I have heard everyone discuss the digression of America, while blaming descending generations and political parties. That is simply not the case. Blaming the descending generations only means the previous generation is disappointed with their own efforts, or set a bad example. Blaming the other party is part of the delusion. In my lifetime, I've heard many conservatives blame the boomers and the "liberals," because we are frequently one in the same, although not always. These groups are blamed for everything from a bad hair day to the price of tea in China. No doubt, there has been a decline in morality at the leadership of an unG-dly agenda, but there are no clear facts that an unG-dly agenda is exclusively in the hands of one party. I truly don't see this as a two party matter at all, but rather another sign of the times.

Many of the baby boomers realized, to the chagrin of the previous generations and in spite of the demand of the descending generations, the historical time of amassing was coming to a close. The bottom line is simple. The world has run out of new land to conquer and claim. Money and material possessions are all that can be amassed at this point. Some boomers have "bought into that" and succeeded , some have "bought into it" at the expense of other's, while still other boomers have simply dropped out and taken the "buy outs." And a few boomers have simply abandoned man's solutions, altogether. I believe my generation clearly exhibit's the Scriptural fact that there are four kinds of people.

If this truly was a political matter of liberal vs. conservative, or democrat vs. republican, the last 50 years would most likely have produced different results. In the fifty years I've been on this earth, there have been only 20 years of Democratic presidents, leaving 30 years with a Republican leader at the helm. I realize there was a Democratic House for many years through that time, but the Senate has gone back and forth, and the Supreme Court has been primarily appointed by Republican Presidents for these same years. Regardless of elections and campaign rhetoric, things do not change for the better with a change of party. We simply develop more areas of disagreement. I cannot speak for the politics of other nations, but in a two party system with three branches of government, we have turned "checks and balance" into "name calling and blame."

Throughout history, there is an obvious pattern that nations maintain a direction of descent, because nothing remains the same and man does not achieve righteousness by legislation, regardless of party leaders. Therefore, with humanity in control, there is no place to go, but down. The blame lies right where it always has, in the rebellious, selfish heart of humanity, which always wants to possess more for self and cast blame elsewhere.

We devote a great deal of time to listening to talk

radio, watching TV, and surfing the net. We are information junkies, and believe ourselves to be informed; yet we allow these sources of blame and bias, much more time than we spend seeking G-d. While humanity is distracted with casting blame, the enemy is continuing his universally, nonpartisan destructive plan . . .

And the destruction of the transgressors and of the sinners shall be together, and they that forsake YHWH shall be consumed.   *Isaiah 1: 28*

And the fruit of your soul's desire has gone from you, and all things delicate and shining have come to an end and will never again be seen.   *Revelation 18: 14*

Chapter 15

The Blame Game

The tactical strategy for the conquest and occupation by the government of the Beast is to divide and conquer. Divide and conquer, then ignite those who are being divided and conquered to blame, blame, blame; each other. We know this is Scriptural from the beginning. The enemy hasn't changed his tactics. He didn't approach Adam and Eve together, did he? The dragon in the Revelation is the same serpent that invaded the garden in Genesis, the shape-shifter, whose identity and intent truly doesn't change. When the knowledge was sought, the fruit was eaten, and they were held to account; Eve blamed the serpent, Adam blamed both Eve and G-d, but the deed was done, all were guilty, and the world was forever changed. Blame did not change the outcome. We don't know whose foot exited the garden first, but we do know, remaining in the garden was forbidden.

G-d is The Creator, therefore it would follow, the enemy is not creative, he does the same thing over and over and over again. I don't like to give recognition to the enemy, because even bad attention is attention, but I have been led to shed just a bit of light on his dark methods. Deception and blame was his *modus operandi* in the Garden. Scripture tells us, it continues to be. Although there is in fact a global government on the horizon, I am of course, addressing these issues from an American perspective. We can read any headline, most any day and see that divisions and uprisings are happening around the globe. I am a citizen of the United States and I don't like the fact that our country is divided on so many issues. Sadly, as the continuation of the Roman Empire, we enjoy and actually feed off of this feuding frenzy. The distraction of blame and opposition over the details, leaves us so vulnerable to the maneuvers of the actual enemy.

Red BLAMEs Blue . . . Blue BLAMEs Red.
Americans know this is not a reference to a ball game, although it does bear many striking resemblances. Perhaps that is because much of the power of the conservative extremism is a voice that began in baseball. This provides the color coordination for hateful, civilized opposition, politically. It seems to be a fairly new game here in America, but the reality is, it's far from new. The "colorful" civilizing of hatemongering may date as far back in American history as to reference the Native Redskins and the Descendants of 'wanted to be' European Blueblood. It was apparent through the Civil War, as the colors blue and grey clearly defined where someone stood. Back to our game of the present. It's become so much a part of our culture that Republican politicians frequently wear red ties and Democrats, blue.

When there is some sort of bipartisan statement or overture to be made, the Republican can sometimes be seen sporting a light blue shirt, or there will be red design in the tie of a Democrat. I'm guessing it's from the foundational concept of the basis for the handshake. An empty hand outstretched indicated, no weapon, so wearing some color of the opposition appears to symbolize bipartisanship or nonpartisanship. I'm not sure our politics ever become that friendly or disarmed, but the colors make it easy to recognize the playing field.

I associate red with anger and aggression, but blue is sometimes a mood and often, the color of the sky. It would seem, if the colors indicate the politics, red is at least more consistent. It is easier to know what to expect and prepare for, when the choices are anger or aggression as opposed to being sad and blue or pie in the sky.

Blacks BLAME and/or fear Whites.
Whites BLAME and/or fear Blacks.

This is what we always revert to, since we have come such a long way and we are such a sophisticated people. The racial issue is still not resolved in America. If anything, it is becoming more of an issue as people seek to be politically correct on the subject of racism. To be honest, I was even concerned as to which order I should list this subheading, to be correct. People are proud of their heritages. I don't know as much about other countries, because I don't live there, and most other countries were not established as a melting pot, but we read every day that there are other areas of prejudice around the world. We know prejudice exists throughout the world regarding nationality, religion, even income, but here in America, we've tried to legislate integration and called it desegregation, or the other way around.

In the attempt to desegregate, much has been lost along

the way, and yet many of the hearts have truly not changed. As I have stated, this is not simply a racial issue. Race is just an easy target here in America. This happens in any situation in which people are forced into some sort of restrictive sameness. Education, economics, and desegregation have not changed the inward perspective.

I have Native American ancestry, and I love the fact that my complexion reflects my heritage. I don't mind, at all, not matching everyone. I'm not a member of the DAR, the Country Club, or the NAACP; nor do I receive a check from the Casino or Bureau of Indian Affairs. And I just don't blame a soul for any of that. G-d made all colors of skin, one is not better or less than another. I have no desire to be a member of anything that excludes another based upon pigment, nor do I want to subsidize or be subsidized based upon that same superficial standard.

There are still whites who use disparaging terms, and there are blacks that openly harbor prejudice, and self-justify. Of course, most any racial comment by a white person, brings Al Sharpton and Jesse Jackson out in full force, which translates to immense verbiage and media coverage. These two men are usually referred to as Rev., but I've yet to hear them discuss the topic of forgiveness or the Good News. The situation of racial equality in this country is really never about being equal, it's always about one or the other failing or at fault.

We seem to fight racism with racism. I've been fascinated in coming to understand this from a Biblical perspective. G-d's Word does not distinguish the human race by pigment, but rather by beliefs. Moses married an Ethiopian woman, so clearly G-d's definition of "mixed marriage" is not the same that our culture has defined and come to recognize. Actually, Scripture even states that Torah was given to a mixed multitude, not just the children of Israel. The term mixed multitude signifies both those that are of the twelve tribes of Israel and those that chose to leave Egypt, an African nation, after recognizing the hand of G-d through the plagues. The second chapter of Acts presents a lengthy list of nationalities gathered for the Feast of Shavu'ot, also known as the Day of Pentecost.

Since humanity was made from the dust of the earth, it's just a matter of varying shades of dirt. I'm pretty much in the middle of the pigment continuum. I once painted an experiment and the results were illuminating. I purchased an oil paint by number kit of Leonardo DaVinci's "Last Supper," and I'd like to share the fascinating facts that I learned in my experiment. As most of us are aware, there are 13 faces around the table, across that painting. In looking at the pre-numbered spaces, each face had three different colors to be painted for proper shading. Rather than paint them all by the designated numbers, I decided to start at one end of the painting with the three lightest colors, which made the first disciple appear very European, even Nordic. I then proceeded to replace the lightest shade of paint with one tone darker on each face as I went across the painting. By the time I reached the other end of the painting, the disciple on the right was a black man. Each face at the table was only one shade, in three, different from the man on either side of him, but the gentlemen at opposite ends reflected a stark difference.

The other thing I learned, just like all "artists," my rendition of Messiah, had the same skin tone I do. Since pigment is only skin deep, I have no idea why racial prejudice is a problem all the way to the core.

Citizens BLAME the Government.

The Government BLAMEs the Circumstances.

There are many governments and circumstances in which revolution, captivity, and military coups settle the disputes. Ours is much more civilized. We must realize that a democratic government allows the freedom for the citizens to voice their complaints, and for that I'm grateful. Although America uses the term democracy, and claims to establish democracies, America is not a democracy. America is a Constitutional republic. There are many nations with constitutions and many nations that claim to be republics.

Russia, Iran, and Venezuela refer to their government's as republics, just to mention a few. A government that "allows" freedom certainly doesn't come free, and the concept is actually an oxymoron, anyway. To refer to being allowed implies permission required and does not actually reflect the true definition of freedom.

Because any large group of people cannot individually self define their society without a stable government, and for a government to be stable, there must be a legal standard. Our Bill of Rights was written to preserve our freedom and keep the government accountable to the people. So, I guess, as a taxpayer, I'd like to "get my money's worth" from the Bill of Rights, and freely share my views. As a believer in Scripture, I believe in choice. I believe choice is everyone's G-d given right. Unfortunately, consequences are a direct result of choice and that's where this blame game becomes established. It is easy for the citizens of this country to blame our government, and yet the citizens are often willing to leave many of their freedoms and choices to the whim of public opinion and popular causes, and continue to elect power hungry, financially unsound leaders.

When the time finally comes to pay the fiddler, the

people have a meek, weak, bleak 'revolution' in the voting booth and scramble the parties. Then we have the solution. The judicial branch schedules hearings for the next year, then takes a break before the hearings commence. Congress blames the Executive branch. The Executive branch blames Congress. And that is the political freedom of a republic espousing democracy, in action!

Pundits BLAME the "Libs."
Public Broadcasting BLAMEs Corporations.
Talk Radio BLAMEs the Media?????

"News/Talk" Radio has to be one of the biggest marketing, programming ploys ever conceived in the mind of man. What a marketing concept! Whomever realized this and brought it to fruition, deserves the millions and bazillions this idea has brought in! There are literal fortunes being amassed to do nothing more than the hawking of political programming. We know this is a marketing bonanza in this country, because many of these men have all made similar comments when callers ask them to run for office. The answer is "Don't want to take the cut in salary."

Patriotism truly does have a cost, and most prefer to talk about their patriotism as to pay the actual price. Even better than giving lip service to one's own patriotism is to discuss at length and repeatedly, someone else's patriotic failings. Aggressive abasing is big money in America, and that somehow gets translated to positive patriotism.

Was this concept born of radio broadcasting through World War II with Tokyo Rose and Tokyo Mose? I've attempted to listen to "News/Talk Radio;" and the length of the shows, alone, is mind-numbing. I just can't quite receive enjoyment from the metaphorical mind set of

121

being a hungry lion waiting day after day, at the same time for the raw meat to be thrown into my cage. I don't want to be one of the thousands or millions assuaged in the cage, I want freedom. Of course, there are always the carefully screened listeners that call in, to let us know what the listening audience is thinking. From what I have heard, and that's not much, most of the listeners are not thinking much more than I'm listening, but rather, are being programmed and actively participating in history revision. I must interject at this point, there is no screening on the Alan Colmes Show. He really does respond to live comments from both sides of the aisle or ends of the fray.

In writing and researching this book, I spent some time listening to News/Talk Radio with an attitude of condescension, which made me a participant, so I completed my research and turned it off. I only listened to an hour of anyone, but in that time, I did get to the place that I liked to hear who and what they were promoting to their audience. I wanted to know what the people who believe they are the most informed, are being told to believe. I don't have to listen to three hours of repeated clips of worst moments and stupid comments by opposing party politicians and the commentary that follows, to develop an opinion. I just want to have a general idea of what we may be facing after the next election.

Although, I'm not a great Clinton fan, I do believe most of the conservative pundits have enjoyed very lucrative careers and much fame by granting commentary to their audiences on the political careers and personal lives of the Clintons. It's as though the Clintons have actually helped make wealthy celebrities of verbose conservatives.

In all fairness, there have been other liberals that have helped, but not as notoriously or as frequently. News/

Talk Radio needs someone to talk about, someone to blame, and a gullible listening audience. America has all those components, as did Japan in the early 40's, before they lost the war.

Kids BLAME Parents.
Parents BLAME the World and Education.
And some Parents BLAME the Kids.

I grew up hearing what a great and free childhood my parents had and what a bad, scary world it had become "out there" by the time I came along. I'm 50 and my parents are still in their 60's, so we've been lead to believe it apparently happened fast! Now, as a middle aged adult, I hear and read what a horrible world it is out there, and I think, "has it changed?" I know it has intensified, but the change itself was a gradual erosion of society for many years. What were once isolated incidents when I was growing up are now daily headlines.

What has truly changed is the erosion of Scriptural values. Those values began to change long ago, and it has taken awhile for the evil to truly be seen. For years, now, here in America, the majority of the population has worked their beliefs around their priorities, and the results have been quite damaging. It's taken over two hundred years, but it's happened. It happened so slowly and so gradually, it went virtually unnoticed, until the point of no return. Which brings us to current events.

In the statement that kids blame parents, an entire pseudo science has taken over the minds of our citizenry and made non-responsible victims of nearly everyone. I'm not saying everyone is now irresponsible, but rather the teaching has been instilled and nurtured to have a certain area or areas of one's life that they are simply a result of their environment. They had no control and now the rest of the world must work around their issues. This did not begin with the boomers. I remember listening to the people born around the turn of the century speaking about practically raising themselves and doing without. Did they actually have it worse than their contemporaries or simply by comparing that standard to the later times? And just what standard defines worse? Those at the turn of the century who enjoyed great freedom and opportunities with little education, but not a great deal of material possessions, or those that were taught materialism makes captivity comfortable?

Parents want to blame the education system for what their children are being taught . . . Teach them better at home. Here it is, over forty years since prayer was officially taken out of American schools and we can still hear it was at the hand of one woman. Where would our nation be now, if all the G-d fearing parents had removed their children from public education, when prayer was removed? I can't count the number of times I've heard and the number e-mails I've received addressing some version of the statement, "They took G-d out of the schools." Why in the world would any G-d fearing parent send their children into a place they believe is G-d forsaken?

As a religious person, I'm glad they have removed religion from the public school system. I think false teachings are more damaging than no teachings. Religion and values need to be taught in the home, not left to the teachers. It's just so much easier to cast blame than take responsibility on all sides of this issue. If kids had a bad childhood, quit wallowing. If they had a good one, then share that goodness. If parents don't like what's being taught, teach otherwise at home or thank G-d, we do still have the option for home schooling. As for the world, it is getting to be a pretty crazy, chaotic place. Home should be a refuge.

Education BLAMEs Ignorance.
And Ignorance simply Exists.

I like this one, because it is just so simple. Our
education system quit teaching kids to think, ages ago,
and began programming ideology. Education chooses to
blame something that can't blame back . . . Pretty smart!
The one draw back. As education has evolved, it has
become it's own enemy. Education is now breeding
ignorance. Kids aren't learning the basics upon which to
build. They are being programmed. And children are not
encouraged in the gifts G-d gave them, but rather are
being pushed and manipulated into achievement of scores
to ensure teacher's tenure, federal funding, and to gain a
piece of paper that will enable them to earn lots of green
paper.

Education is operating in ignorance. When I read that
a kindergartener was handcuffed for a tantrum, I thought
the teacher, the cops, and the parents should all be
reprimanded. What in the world is wrong with the grown-
ups in this picture? Now, the hard line disciplinarians
will shout about "sparing the rod and spoiling the child"
and proclaim the problem to be a lack of corporal
punishment. And to those that smack us all up the side of
the head with child rearing quotes from the book of
Proverbs, the book in the Bible that teaches how to get
along with the rest of humanity, I would simply ask them
if they live by the same law they enforce. Children don't
know what to do, the boundaries are strange and the
consequences are inconsistent. Parents that use the Bible
to punish their child while excusing themselves from
literal Scriptural obedience, are simply provoking their
children to reject G-d and discipline. Which brings us
back to kindergarteners in handcuffs.

Obviously there were situations prior to this one, in which someone may have seen a red flag or warning sign. If the child has been in child care prior to school, where is the record? If the child has been home with mom all these years before school, where and what was the social preparation? At any rate, she's already been educated with an experience of a lifetime that has probably only served to desensitize the possible consequences of truancy, shop lifting or experimentation with drugs or alcohol. She's already been arrested, handcuffed, and detained! What has our education system already taught her about our legal system, in kindergarten?

Patients BLAME Life.
Doctors BLAME Disease or Insurance and now Patients . . .

I read this week, as I'm writing this book that doctors are now having to "fire" their patients, so I had to add patients to the list of difficulties, doctors must deal with. Their patients are just too obnoxious, bringing in Internet information and challenging the doctor's diagnosis, prognosis and treatment plan. Imagine, some patients have actually ceased to view doctors as gods! Yet I've actually heard doctors give web addresses for health references. Included in another chapter is an example of a doctor giving a web address for patients to utilize, but he was specific as to which link he would recommend to his patients, when he is too busy to answer all their questions.

Just a few short years ago, doctors were blaming lawyers for helping their patients hold them accountable, and before that, according to those in the medical profession, it was the insurance companies that made life difficult. Could it be that doctors just don't like to be questioned or held in account?

I remember when a number of doctors put their

"practices of compassion for humanity" on hold to run for public office and push tort reform through. Once that was done, the patients are still not as submissive to their "authority" as they should be, and so now, patients are apt to be fired. I find this ludicrous.

Let me present my perspective from a purely economic standpoint. Doctors are paid by the patient, the patient's insurance company, or the government, which is paid for by the patient, their employment, or the taxpayers. So, regardless of how it's explained and covered, doctors work for the patient. Doctors are like subcontractors or simply contract labor for a specific "event."

If the doctor doesn't want to do the job, he/she has every right to quit or resign, but no one, not even doctors who think they are a god, can fire the ones who pay them. Doctors work for their patients or the insurance companies or the government. If a doctor can fire his patient, then the doctor isn't working for the patient. It truly is as simple as that. Most everyone with health issues knows a poor diet and high stress adds to the symptoms or aggravates the illness. So, rather than start with simplifying in both areas, people now increase their stress level by paying to be treated with condescension, in fear their treatment could be halted at any point.

In-laws BLAME In-laws.

What else can be said? It's always amazed me at just how much autonomy a particular member of a family is judged to be "allowed." Many times families meddle and disapprove of the spouse of their family member. They don't approve of the changes in their loved one. They don't approve of the politics, the religion, the career, or the cooking of the spouse. The list of just how the in-law fails, can be quite lengthy, or it can be only one issue, but a major one. And by the same token, the list of points of disapproval by a spouse, simply tells their partner, they don't approve of the people from which they hail.

When families display their disapproval or when spouses display theirs, it is nothing more than a total disregard of the person that makes both sides of the in-law relationship, related. When a man's family disapproves of his wife or advises him extensively, the wife very quickly wonders why her husband is so undeserving of respect. She may at first blame the in-laws, but ultimately she will begin to cast glances of judgment upon the man she married. In that same manner, when a woman is disregarded by a man's family, she will ultimately feel unprotected by her mate.

When a man observes difficult interaction between his wife and her family, he knows it's only a matter of time until the only way to keep peace in his home is to disregard his in-laws. These particular familial interactions were prophesied in the New Testament, as well as clear Instruction given in the second chapter of Genesis. When G-d joins a couple, the two are one, and the man, in order to maintain the respect G-d has ordained for him, must establish himself as the head of a new household.

When in-laws stoop to blaming the in-law in protection of their family member, they are simply stating that their loved one does not make good decisions and should be disrespected and disregarded, as they are demonstrating. As to the old adage, "blood is thicker than water . . ." Not according to Scripture. According to Scripture, no one is to come between a man and his wife, and that directive covers many more individuals than adulterers and divorce court judges. It says no human, which covers the marriage partners themselves, in-laws, children, and commiserating friends. This is probably why the enemy uses so many in close proximity, attempting to accomplish this endeavor.

Wives BLAME Husbands,
Husbands BLAME Talk Shows.
Women enter a dark slippery slope of camaraderie when they decide to try to identify with others about their personal life, or when they open themselves up to vain imaginings of how it should be . . . The women that are not working outside the home are a minority to begin with. Add the special blend of the talk show subliminal message of unfulfilled and we find the recipe for disaster and the equation for dissatisfaction. The talk shows are full of advice and commentary for what a good relationship should be and of course, the ever feared signs of a bad relationship.

Women who work outside the home have even more temptation, I think, to contemplate and doubt. First, there is the drive time every day that gives them time to reflect. Depending upon the traffic, the reflection time can focus on dinner plans or the last argument, but a woman's mind is rarely in neutral and woman are simply hardwired to be focused on the home front. Next she has her coworkers that range from young and single to middle aged and divorced to older and possibly widowed, and the exception to the rule, happily married. Talk happens, it just does, whether it's at the drinking fountain, over lunch, or smoking in the cold with the other lepers of the 21st century. Children, spouses, money troubles, and good times get discussed along the way. It seems most people are always going through something and when these things start being compared, even though for the most part, it's apples and oranges, a dissatisfaction with life begins to set in. When the attitude of dissatisfaction gets aimed at the marriage, the 'logical' solution is to blame the situation, which leads to blaming the spouse.

For women, when stress becomes overwhelming or unhappiness is entertained, a better husband or a husband on better behavior would resolve the problem, therefore; the husband is to blame. Add a bad Lifetime movie, with ads from daytime TV, to that equation and it takes no time at all to confirm the notion that life needs to change, beginning with him. It is interesting to note that most husbands don't really take all this blame too seriously. They invariably chalk up the dissatisfaction to other influences ranging from hectic schedules to hormones, but it isn't them. Husbands believe they have to be trying to make a wife miserable to be responsible for her misery and since they aren't aiming at that, it can't be them. There is a certain confident logic to that line of thinking, which will ultimately only cause him further blame.

Husbands BLAME Hormones.
Wives BLAME Sports, TV or Work.

Men are not usually so vocal in their dissatisfaction with life. They usually demonstrate their frustration in a displacement style or pecking order arrangement. Wives are demanding by nature and just like men, not usually at fault, by their own assessment. Most wives will tell you otherwise, in a round about sort of avoidance, but it's the avoidance and the need to explain and blame that will leave her wondering and searching and looking for what is making her husband frustrated, disinterested, grouchy, or all the above. The first solution a wife nearly always entertains is all the other things that keep a husband from happily tending to quality time with her and or the family.

Men like to spend time where they feel they are in control of their destiny. Some men find that at work, some find it in the wilderness, some find it in their workshop or den and some have simply given up to stare at the TV. I'm not suggesting the sports fans have given up on life, actually quite to the contrary. If they were the quarter back or the center or the coach, the game would go as such and the team would win. The problem most women have difficulty understanding, is the difference between men and women. Women are somehow completed and fulfilled, even defined by her role as a wife, which brings her interaction with her husband into part of the central focus of her life.

A man, on the other hand, has a wife because it's not good for man to be alone, according to the Word of G-d. So when he's done with his priorities and he's not wanting to be alone, then and only then is her definition of quality time a major factor. That is not an indicator that he doesn't love the woman he's married to, he's just got other things to do. There are no more countries to conquer, so there's hunting, and building, and designing, and drafting, or wood cutting, or gardening, or a myriad of things that must be accomplished for him to be the hunter, protector, and provider. Quality time isn't what a relationship is about from a man's perspective, except of course, the men that have been conquered by the pop psychology culture that dominates afternoon TV.

Most men don't have to constantly analyze their life to be happy, they just have to be living it in a way that gives them some sense of accomplishment. As a rule, women prefer interaction and men prefer accomplishment. Survival used to be one of the bonds that held a couple together. When life was truly dependent upon a couple working together to have food and shelter for the winter, there was a bond that simply wouldn't break, or couldn't break. There wasn't much time for feeling unfulfilled and under appreciated. There are exceptions, however; and when that happens, both parties in that relationship are reversed, so the difference for the dance still exists.

There is one subject that invariably draws a couple to admit the same issue, while agreeing to blame the other. It seems to the biggest issue the American family faces, and from the headlines will continue to face for sometime. Now that survival appears to depend upon two incomes, but rarely are two people joined in their goals, the bond has become financial blame.   This blame game will likely continue, because now in this economy, who can afford a divorce?

People BLAME Almost Everyone and Everything
Married women blame single women, single women blame percentages. Divorced women blame their ex. Married men blame marriage and obligation. Single men blame time. Divorced men blame feminism. Working mothers blame the high cost of living.

In all of this, the one thing everyone has in common, which will serve as the "common ground" to commiserate in the next relationship, is the lack of individual responsibility or self accountability.

I could go into great detail regarding the 'greener pastures beyond the fence syndrome,' and the social bonds that form as a result of failed and absent relationships. But one sentence says it so succinctly, to elaborate would only distract from the message. We comfort ourselves with a simple yet totally untrue concept.
It's someone else's fault my life doesn't meet my expectations!

Philosophy BLAMES Theology.
Theology BLAMES heathens.
There is nothing more abstract and foundationally intangible than philosophy, and yet it's adherents contemplate and contemplate and contemplate their own

ever evolving views while condemning and judging those that would insist upon consistency in their thoughts and beliefs. That is not to say, we should remain insistent upon illogic and call it faith or insist upon ignorance when confronted with insight, but I'm always amazed at the philosopher's rejection of Scripture while clinging to his own impalpable perceptions or insights of abstruse concepts.

To establish a course of life and establish ethics, while removing G-d's Word, is nothing more than anti-Theology, which is the basic foundation of philosophy. Philosophy, by definition, is humanistic ethics, without G-d included; which is anti-theistic. In all of the blame game being played, I believe this to be one of the most spiritually dangerous, as philosophy has been cleverly woven into the fabric of cultures around the world.

Philosophy is nothing more than the elevation of man's ideas and concepts for living, as in the deceptive promise in the Garden of Eden. The serpent offered Eve the gift of philosophy, "to know what G-d knows, while disregarding what HE said."

Theology blames "heathens" and when that happens, we know there is something unacceptable about the theology. G-d blames sin and He's not happy with heathens that choose sin, but He is equally unhappy with theologians that barricade heathens from access to the truth. HIS Son called them vipers.

BLAME for the Sake of BLAME

Animal protection groups will continue to rise and so will animal disease control, because that will be a leading issue in the One World Government. What we see now, is like looking through a keyhole, as to the control and issues that will be mandated regarding animals in the beastly government. Controlling people through animals is a predominant plank in the platform of this horrendous monocracy. We see this on a very small scale here in our country with PETA, the USDA, and now NAIS. PETA is the organization that tends to oversee the 'care' of animals by projecting human feelings upon them and pretty much blames meat eaters. So, of course, reciprocally, the meat lovers blame PETA.

Historically, long before there was PETA there have been people who referred to their dogs as family members and in ancient cultures, cats were deified. So once again, as Scripture says, "there is nothing new under the sun." Elevating the value of animals over people has been done for thousands of years. It's just that now, there is an organization to either promote or blame. Interestingly this is even becoming political, in that there are more vegetarians amongst liberals, while the conservatives tend to be meat eaters. Granted there are exceptions to this observation, myself included. It would appear that ultimately, at least in America, every issue will be micro-dissected in an effort to maintain political division. Since the D in USDA stands for the word, department, this is a bureaucratic arm of the government. Being a bureaucracy gives the USDA authority without a reason, or the authority to make the reason.

Conservation agents have much more control than any not for profit organization ever will. It is the arm of the government that controls man's access to the land, water, and wild life. This power has grown in a relatively short time, to the point a conservation agent can search your deep freeze looking for contraband pelts or illegal game. This is based on the ever increasing popular notion of our government, that we are all potential criminals. So, the hunters blame gun control and civilization rather than poachers and invasive government. The ecologists blame the hunters, rather than studying history and realizing the original inhabitants helped maintain the eco-system through hunting. If only the Indians had received the same protection against extinction that the wolf and eagle have received!

In the state of Texas, there is a law on the books that justifies deadly force to protect private property, yet the farmer and rancher are prohibited from protecting their livestock from "protected" predators. Just what sort of civilization would lobby for a law that determines private property to be more important than human life, while the private property of livestock is of less value than a wild predator? The international headlines indicate there is even less respect for the lives, rights, and freedom of the citizens in many other countries.

While addressing conservation and ecology, we must address the fact that there is Federal Protection of certain predators . . . This is not the act of PETA, but the Federal Government, and there are other regulations in place in other countries. Protecting predators will ultimately work to control and contain the food supply and access in any nation. When the food supply is centrally controlled, the citizens are much more apt to become compliant and be willing to receive special ID for the buying and selling of what they need.

I do believe this drive to not unite may have some basis in spiritual discernment. We don't want to become part of the big One World Order. So the human solution is to unite to divide. If opposition remains divisive, unification is presumed impossible. And yet, in our human insight which is so limited, the cohesive groups are being conquered while seeking divisiveness.

All this blame is simply exhaustive and leading the entire population of the globe to a universal "choice." In all this blame, who takes responsibility? Obviously, in all this blame, someone needs to establish morality and good decisions for the majority. Just writing about these few examples in this chapter, I found myself completely and mentally exhausted. What has casting blame in regard to any of these subjects, accomplished?

So, while the world continues to go 'round, and the wheels continue to squeak, there has already been introduced; a standard of laws that will, in the beginning, appeal to all peoples . . . With the exception of a ridiculed fanatical few.

And the very G-d of peace sanctify you wholly; and I pray G-d your whole spirit and soul and body be preserved blameless unto the coming of our Lord Y'hshuwah Messiah.

I Thessalonians 5: 23

So if one is blameless, they are without blame.
Does that mean:

    A. They are forgiven by G-d
    B. Innocent, regardless of human accusations
    C. They do not cast blame and accusations?
    D. All of the above?

My G-d hath sent his angel, and hath shut the lions' mouths, that they have not hurt me: forasmuch as before him innocency was found in me; and also before thee, O king, have I done no hurt.

Daniel 6: 22

And I heard another voice from heaven, saying, Come out of her, my people, that ye be not partakers of her sins, and that ye receive not of her plagues.

Revelation 18: 4

Chapter 16

Uniting to Hold Ourselves Blameless

Once in a while, we humans find a way to work together, stop blaming each other for a moment and simply organize a plan that leaves G-d out. This generally happens when something occurs that leaves a considerable number of us victims of "an act of G-d." Clearly by human standard, the concept of repentance is inapplicable in these instances.

Does it seem that we are having more weather than usual? Of course the answer to that question is, no. Weather is simply the condition of the atmosphere, so good or bad, we have weather, however; it does seem that there are more storms and unseasonable weather conditions. Several times in the past few years, be it through the warning or the report of the aftermath, the

137

phrase "of Biblical proportion" has been used to describe the weather event. Anyone can look out the window or read a headline and realize the weather is certainly getting our attention. It's not just outdoors, either. The weather is affecting our lifestyles. Too much snow or ice and we lose our electricity. Not enough rain and the inland water level gets low. Some towns have even rationed water.

I read today, on one of the forums in which I participate, a man stated that after much study and meditation, he was just sure G-d hates our particular geographical locale. I don't believe that G-d hates us, but rather hates the way in which we are choosing to prioritize and conduct our lives. I think I understand his sentiment, and knowing the writings of this individual, I will hazard to say, I've never perceived him to be a religious scholar. Truthfully, I'm sure all this inclement weather is from G-d and for a very specific reason. Whether He's sending it or allowing it, I think He's sending or allowing it in love, still as a warning; rather than judgment. I believe the judgment will be much worse.

In my ministry and travels, I once met a young man that said he was going to be a missionary in another country. He was determined to go to Bible college and be on his way. He already spoke the language of the country in which he was planning to go but . . . Through an interesting turn of events, his enrollment in Bible college began with either a bit of knavery or naiveté. At any rate, by the time he graduated, he had changed his plans and decided to stay stateside and take a religious job, with comfortable accommodations and a nice salary. I've often wondered when I see weather headlines in the town in which he resides, provided he does have a calling, has he done what Jonah did and disobeyed? Is the storm tossing his town, as it did the ship in which Jonah boarded to avoid his call?

Our nation survived the drought of the 1930's by rebellion and government dependence. We didn't, as a nation, turn to G-d. We went to town and continued working on Sabbath. When my Grandma passed away, I received some of the books she and my Grandpa had kept through the years. I was particularly drawn to a teacher's study guide for Sunday School. When I read the special notes to teachers that were teaching teen-agers, it stated something to the effect of, 'Young people today need real direction. They are not just going to accept tradition.' And something else about experiencing new things . . . The copyright date was 1933. Again, the Scripture came to mind, "there is nothing new under the sun." It would appear that the baby boomers were not the first generation to question the establishment, and I pray we are not the last, to do so.

After the crash of the stock market and when the ground produced nothing but dust, a spirit of unreason and panic took this nation by storm. When there were no crops, the people headed to town for jobs. This obviously wouldn't resolve the hunger issue, but rather the matter of "want." Apparently the lack of produce on the farm was never connected with the foodstuffs of the markets and grocery stores, or the potential for the lack of it. If crops would not grow, how would the shelves get stocked? If the ground didn't produce, what would be the diet? Ford fenders and factory rivets from a good town job? It was when science explained the need to obey G-d's Word that the crops began to flourish, once again, although it was not stated in so many words.. G-d's Word is clear that agriculturally, the ground must have a resting season. The term fallow is now, acknowledged and recognized and has already become antiquated throughout farming and agriculture. For a time when science had explained it and our government enforced and subsidized it, we were willing to do what G-d instructed in Torah . . . well in a modernistic, scientific sort of way, with pay and insurance. Now, we have replaced leaving the land lie fallow for a season, with crop rotation. And we can see once again, what is happening to the cost of farming and the cost of groceries.

When obedience to G-d was no longer the concern, and repentance was not the solution, the foundation was thus established to enter the Age of Technology, leading us to the potential Technocracy. We chose to listen to scientists when we neglected to believe G-d or simply rejected HIS Word. How can we be so sure we are exempt from G-d's law, when we must keep writing more laws, for survival?

Unfortunately when we decided, as a society, to become urban dwellers dependant upon scientific evidence and government mandate, we fell right into the exact same situation of those in the book of Genesis. It took less than seven years for the farmers of Pharaoh's Egypt to become sharecroppers and indentured servants, just to have something to eat, stay alive, and to serve the court of Pharaoh, yet another year. The account is accurately recorded in Genesis, right down to ownership and taxation. The majority of our nation did in the 1930s, exactly what was done in Egypt prior to captivity and the Exodus. How was this fact overlooked?

We Now Have the Capability to Ignore the Warning . . . The drought of the 1930s has become historic proof that we can find our way around G-d's warning and without a doubt, have certainly found the alternative to repentance!

Scripture speaks of Enoch walking with G-d, right out of this world. Later we are told that Elijah was caught up in a whirlwind, while Elisha watched . . . I mean no offense or disregard to those who have lost loved ones in weather storms. Could the whirlwind mentioned in

Scripture be what we call a tornado? Is the increase of tornado weather, a possible method of exit or rapture from this world for G-d's people? For all extremists, I'm not suggesting that we go jump in front of a funnel cloud. I'm simply posing a question, for which I do not have the answer. A pillar of cloud in Exodus could easily be seen as a tornado, and to be caught up in a whirlwind, could absolutely describe the effects of a tornado, as in the account of Elijah.

And it came to pass, as they still went on, and talked, that, behold, there appeared a chariot of fire, and horses of fire, and parted them both asunder; and Elijah went up by a whirlwind into heaven.   *II Kings 2: 11*

I realize loss of life in a tornado is tragic, but there are also incomprehensible accounts of survival in tornados that truly do defy explanation.

Could the apparent increase of inclement weather be a direct result of man's attempt to alter and control what has always been exclusively attributed to the power of G-d? Has man's attempt to harness the power of the weather or control it, brought the increase of these turbulent atmospheric conditions? I can't say, but I do know, there is nothing that happens in this world that G-d doesn't either cause or allow.

Have our traditions taught us to fear weather rather than fear G-d, who is the Master and Creator of all things including weather?

Many things happened in Scripture that were "weather related." Sometimes G-d's people were unaffected and other times, the weather completely got their attention, as was meant to happen. Scripture states very clearly that the plagues of Egypt did not affect the area in which the children of Israel were living. G-d also warned that worse things would be seen and endured, if He were ignored by His people. Unfortunately, it seems that humanity continues to make choices in which G-d allows us to walk out the consequences of choices made without His direction and blessing.

It's so easy to see the comparison of Pharaoh's army and Jonah's plight when comparing Scripture to modern day tsunamis and hurricane Katrina, but do we see any possible Scriptural comparisons when weather affects America's Bible belt or Israel? When Israel gave Gaza to the Palestinians, there was discussion and veiled accusations regarding possible sabotage of the farming land. When the land belonged to Israel, it had been used in crop production. When Israel relinquished her land and the greenhouses, produce was simply not as plentiful. Not only have the Palestinians been disappointed in their land acquisition, Israel's economy has suffered, as well. Having visited that part of the world fairly recently, I can attest to the vastness of the desert in that area. Without the favor of G-d, I can't imagine how any agriculture would thrive. G-d's Word says the land in question is to belong to Israel and Israel is not to negotiate with the surrounding peoples.

Deuteronomy 28 very clearly states that G-d will bless HIS people with good produce, when they live according to HIS Word, and the rest of the chapter explains the results when people choose ways other than G-d's. I know, in my own life, when I get outside of G-d's plan, the little piece of earth in which I inhabit changes, sometimes, dramatically. We can also read in Scripture that Job's family was affected in a single day, and Job had not been disobedient, with the possible exception that he harbored fear. I have discovered a very simple fact of life. When I am obedient to G-d's Word, He sends appropriate weather in it's season, or gives me peace through the storm.

Although I'm not so presumptuous or arrogant as to

think my personal behavior necessarily affects the weather for miles around, I cannot assume an irresponsible perspective, either. We know our decisions affect those around us. Everyone on the boat that was carrying Jonah weathered that storm with him. Just like Jonah, servants of G-d are called to be obedient; and disobedience renders chastisement or punishment.

Now that we predict and prophesy regarding weather and conditions and science is boasting of ways to control and cause it, are we crossing lines that we now simply refer to as, technological advancement? I differentiated earlier in this chapter between G-d sending weather and G-d allowing weather for a very important reason. Science is manipulating weather and claiming to be gaining expertise in the area of cloud seeding and rain enhancement. So, as weather reports gain accuracy, could it simply be a case of 'cause and effect?' If science is causing the rainfall, it would only make sense it could be accurately predicted.

There is a Weather Modification Association using the not for profit (.org) and a Weather Modification, Inc. which is of course, (.com). When I did a Google Search, I discovered many states have some sort of program, licensing, or availability through their conservation and education programs. This, naturally, makes me wonder about the possible ramifications that haven't yet been studied, fully. What about the possibility of hurricanes and tornadoes and other severe weather in surrounding areas, or the potential for causing floods when clouds are seeded?

This technology has made it possible for us, as a civilized religious nation to decline participation in something so 'pagan' as rain dancing. If we seek a solution besides G-d, how is that different than heathen cultures that have their rainmakers and rituals? It seems so much more humble and respectful to G-d, to simply believe HE will send rain in it's season, if we live according to HIS Word.

Is there anyone in this country that has shared what they have heard regarding a weather forecast without immediately following the information with a comment pertaining to the inaccuracy of weather forecasts? Yet faith, in the weather report has increased dramatically in the nearly half century that I have been listening, and as technology increases, so does the dependency in knowing the future. I'm not sure when weather forecasting became removed from the category of prophesying, but there are certainly examples of Scriptural prophets giving very accurate weather forecasts. As a matter of fact, if the prophet was not accurate he was labeled and known as a false prophet. To be recognized a false prophet was hardly a matter to be taken lightly. Many today, listen to the weather reports as casually as they read their horoscope or call a psychic. Many listen to weather reports, faithfully, that wouldn't dream of reading a horoscope or calling a psychic.

I'm not condemning the meteorologists or weather persons. What happened to simply trusting G-d about the weather, when HIS Word says so much about the seasons and the rains? I realize our global society is becoming quite transient, but most of us are familiar with the weather in the area in which we live. Why have we chosen to become so dependent upon the forecasts and place our faith in the technological predictions? How does G-d view our hearts? Are we operating in wisdom when we listen to man or are we placing our faith in the knowledge of man?

In the time of writing this book, the area in which I live experienced a horrific tornado. I was inadvertently, outdoors at the time it came through. I know in my heart,

I was not tempting G-d. I hadn't heard any warnings, I could see that the sky was horribly discolored and as a "shepherd" I knew two of our goats didn't have access to the big barn, so I went out to move them. I had no sooner walked out the front door toward the well house, when the rain and hail began. The goats had helped themselves to the porch of the well house and looked as if they were waiting for me to unlock the gate.

I didn't have to lead them, simply unlocked the gate and they ran in the barn lot and into the barn. The wind was too strong for me to make it back to the house, so I stayed up against the outside wall of the well house while watching and listening as the storm moved through on the other side of the bluff. I could hear the sound of the tornado and saw the sky moving so fast, I still can't fully describe what I saw, nor do I have words to describe the devastation that followed.

When did humanity choose to place their trust in the knowledge of man, and refer to faith; as tempting G-d?

For it is written, I will destroy the wisdom of the wise, and will bring to nothing the understanding of the prudent. For after that in the wisdom of G-d the world by wisdom knew not G-d, . . .
                    I Corinthians 1: 19, 20a

YHWH shall open unto thee His good treasure, the heaven to give the rain unto thy land in his season, and to bless all the work of thine hand: and thou shalt lend unto many nations, and thou shalt not borrow. And YHWH shall make thee the head, and not the tail; and

thou shalt be above only, and thou shalt not be beneath;
if that thou hearken unto the commandments of YHWH
thy G-d, which I command thee this day, to observe and
to do them: *Deuteronomy 28: 12, 13*

But thou, O Daniel, shut up the words, and seal the
book, even to the time of the end: many shall run to and
fro, and knowledge shall be increased.
                                   Daniel 12: 4

Saying, Hurt not the earth, neither the sea, nor the trees,
till we have sealed the servants of our G-d in their
foreheads.
                                   Revelation 7: 3

Chapter 17

The Religion of
Nationalism

Nationalism is the belief system that allows the basic tenets of all three religions, yet unfortunately keeps their adherents in their place of intimidation and in fearful unquestioning compliance.

I've continued to inquire of YHWH as I've been writing this book, and keep hearing the portion of the account of the Gospel that states " . . . *if it were possible, they shall deceive the very elect.*" Once I changed and sought from the perspective that so very many of us are so very certain we are not deceived, I began to gain a new understanding.

The world religion and government will not be one religion or one government taking over all the other religions and governments, but rather a reversal and inclusion of what we now recognize as religion and/or government.

Nationalism has all the zeal and emotional fervor of a religion, it's all intertwined. The Muslims have declared war on their definition of infidels. The Christians exercise their military might citing Old Testament Scriptures and although Israel is not a mono-theocracy at this point in history, they define their humanly ordained democracy to be "chosen." Clearly the passion and fervor of each group, are for a comfortable culture with religious rights for self-fulfillment, based upon their identity as a people or nation.

The Muslims don't hate America for it's religious beliefs. Religious beliefs are quite varied in this country, and for some Americans, non-existent. The more vocal Muslims refer to America's materialistic culture as abhorrent and those that defend it to the death of others, to be infidels. Although violence is not the answer, they are not completely wrong in their view of materialism . . .The Muslims are unquestioningly living up to what the G-d of Israel said they would do and be. They are war-mongering and unwilling and unable to get along, even with each other. Each faction believes they should have the control. The sons of Ishmael, as the Arab nations, continue to prove the Words of the living G-d of Israel. G-d is not wrong in HIS description.

Israel, on the other hand, is openly deceived and being further deceived. The Roadmap to Peace eliminates them from the global map more efficiently than a military attack from Lebanon or Iran. Every uproarious step of concession in the Roadmap to Peace, falsely portrays to the rest of the world, Israel as the villainous occupier. The Roadmap to Peace has only served to further isolate Israel from the rest of the world, while that small nation continues to make further concessions at the urging of what appears to be her only ally. Now that America is perceived in a negative way throughout most of the world, the possibility for Israel to be held in account as an ally, grows stronger. G-d has already warned, in HIS Word, the results Israel will bring upon itself as a nation if land negotiations occur.

There are many commemorations and events to pay homage to patriotism and nationalism. In the listing of local events, there are numerous civic festivals and parades, honoring different historical events and groups deemed important to our community or nation. Most of these parades and celebrations take place on Saturday, and are frequently war or military related. Saturday is translated nearly around the world, from the word Sabbath, the day G-d set apart and called holy. Schools have patriotic pageants, but not religious celebrations. Some might place the events and respectful deference in the category of worship! My grandchildren get specified days off each month of the school year, except April. There is no recognition of Passover or Easter, no long week-ends, absolutely nothing. April is the only month on their school calendar that has no school holidays. I remember very clearly when my little elementary school granddaughters had their big patriotic pageant on the last day before "spring break." There are two immense issues with that concept of spring break in elementary school. First, they are to young to go to Ft. Lauderdale or Padre! Second, what kind of message is being sent when there is a patriotic pageant right before a week break in the spring? Seems to place this spring break right up there with Christmas vacation, which is now called winter holiday.

I do not pledge allegiance to anything or anyone but G-d. Many would say that makes me unpatriotic. I'm not running for office and I love the people of this country, but just as Daniel was forced to make a decision, we must also recognize the line between reasonable expected

149

respect, and worship. The day is coming in which we will all need to know where that line is drawn.

Wrong theocracy still operates in spiritual strength and that is stronger than military might. Scripture is the only strength in dealing with those that have declared a "holy war!"

Discounting the statutes of Scripture and making materialism a god; is by definition, idolatry, heathenism, or pagan. Those that adhere to materialism are frequently referred to as infidels. Infidel is not just a term used by Middle Eastern leaders to describe the Western culture. Scripture also uses the term. The difference between the spelling and pronunciation in the Greek between the two words, apostle and infidel, is shockingly minimal. But Scripture also says, our faith is shown, not in words, but deeds.

We can see in our own nation that national holidays have certainly superseded G-d's Holy Days. We can read John's account of the Gospel and Paul's determination to return to Jerusalem after his conversion to realize, G-d's Holy Days are still to be observed. When one cites Colossians 2: 16 to be excused from such holy celebrations, they are certainly not to be replaced with national holidays or other "religious observances." The book of John carefully gives a detailed outline of Messiah celebrating all of G-d's Holy Days.
John 3: 16 is everyone's invitation to join Him.

Let us not kid ourselves or be deceived, in this religion of nationalism, human sacrifice still takes place in the form of war.

Ye have heard that it hath been said, Thou shalt love thy neighbour, and hate thine enemy. But I say unto you, Love your enemies, bless them that curse you, do good to them that hate you, and pray for them which

despitefully use you, and persecute you;
                                        Matthew 5: 43, 44

As it is written in the law of Moses, all this evil is come
upon us: yet made we not our prayer before YHWH our
G-d, that we might turn from our iniquities, and
understand thy truth.
                                        Daniel 9: 13

I know thy works, and thy labour, and thy patience, and
how thou canst not bear them which are evil . . .
Nevertheless I have somewhat against thee, because
thou hast left thy first love. Remember therefore from
whence thou art fallen, and repent, and do the first
works; or else I will come unto thee quickly, and will
remove thy candlestick out of his place, except thou
repent.
                                        Revelation 2 : 2a, 4, 5

Chapter 18

Direction and Purpose

According to Scripture, the will of man is usually at odds with the Will of G-d; therefore a government that is "great, by virtue of the will of the people" cannot really be a G-dly nation. How can the laws of man possibly override the laws of G-d? America is living proof that man cannot make enough laws to remove man's free choice to do evil. I read that Saudi Arabia actually has a law on the books and is enforced by religious police regarding the walking of pets. It is their opinion that men and women use pets to meet those of the opposite sex. Humanity, even well meaning, just doesn't have the integrity or ethics to maintain justice by it's own definition. So, on to my point.

It seems this political rhetoric that always accompanies

any issue is masking the truth. Rewriting history to appear G-dly isn't really going to change anything, except to keep the constituents looking at all the "scenery." When President Bush ran against Al Gore, the Republicans insisted that the entire nation realize that we are a republic, not a democracy, and they are correct. So the debate between republic and democracy led us to the blue vs. red states to the political civil war in which we continuously participate, to this day. No one seems to realize or acknowledge that our form of government is really being defined as we go. Since we have insisted upon the recognition of the difference between a republic and a democracy, a republic really cannot go around the world and set the example to establish democracies, now can it?

By using the terms, democracy and republic, interchangeably when commodious, but drawing a line of distinction when convenient, we abandon the best of either, and chance creating the worst of both.

Technically, democracy flies in direct opposition to Theocracy, as do empires, republics, and traditional monarchies, as well as communism, totalitarianism, and all other man made governments. Republics, historically tend to be the rebellious offspring of monarchies and/or empires. Nowhere in Scripture is the will of man ever on the same level as the Will of Almighty G-d. So, that removes both America and present day Israel, from the definition of G-dly nations. I mention these two nations specifically, because it is of course, easy to see that other nations are not citing Holy Scripture to profess the ordination and purpose of the Almighty Creator. As a matter of a fact, few nations on earth, other than Israel and America, espouse a direct appointment from the G-d of Scripture, for their presence. We are beginning to hear some of the Muslim world claim divine appointment, but their holy book is not Scripture and it is historically recent. Their inconsistency in war and claim for peace is clear that they are self-defined, rather than divine.

The fact that Israel will be oppressed politically, is a foregone conclusion. Consider the pressure Israel already faces to being "diplomatically eliminated" from the map with land concessions, without any actual overt threat of attack. From where has this pressure come? It was first introduced by Israel's ally in the name of peace and safety, but it is gaining strength and momentum. A world wide unified effort, culminating in the fulfillment of the prophecy in Zechariah 14: 2, which tells us, "All nations will come against Jerusalem." Does this prophecy include Israel, in all nations against Jerusalem? G-d's Word clearly states that Israel is to be a Theocratic monarchy, which at present day, Israel is not. So unless there is serious repentance that has not been prophesied in Scripture, if Israel exists as a nation, Israel will be one of the nations against Jerusalem. The same can be said for the United States. Scripture is clear in Zechariah when it is stated, "all nations." Therefore, there are only two options for the United States in that passage. Either the US ceases to exist before that time of fulfillment, or the US is also one of the nations against Jerusalem.

The government of Israel is actually already faced with negotiations regarding the division of the city of G-d, and without G-d's blessing upon a man made democracy, Israel is once again facing the same inevitability as in the days of Jeremiah. G-d outlined the perimeter of the land and specifically prohibited the negotiation of the land by the children of Israel. Having seen, first hand, the Temple Mount and having been refused access at gun point, I can attest to the fact that the presence of Al-Aqsa Mosque plainly indicates, Jerusalem, to be already divided.

Whether it's the description of Babylon or the

155

consequences of sin, America sees nothing pertinent in the history contained in the book of Jeremiah, and apparently Israel has forgotten.

Those of us following along in the New Testament have tended to read the current State of Israel into all of the passages about the sons of Jacob, the tribes of Israel or the city of Jerusalem. I believe I am to fully support any nation that is protecting and preserving Jerusalem, however; this present State of Israel is not the theocratic nation that G-d has chosen Israel to be, and has not claimed and protected Jerusalem. Obviously, nations that call themselves theocratic that are not based upon Scripture have also missed the definition. Any current European or Western republic, democracy, or even monarchy can trace and claim some connection with the Roman Empire, which according to the book of Daniel will not be totally disestablished until Messiah reigns.

A G-dly democracy is a paradoxical title. Israel does not claim a national religion of Judaism, but Judaic law greatly influences their political scene. Our nation claims religious freedom, which has obviously translated for many, to be freedom from religion. At any rate, a nation that is not governed by G-d's laws cannot be a G-dly nation. There, of course, can be and are G-dly individuals in any nation, including America and Israel.

Now, onto Islam. As varying leaders claim their nations to be theocracies, and technically that is possible, even with false gods and false "holy" books, but the results are a false theocracy. Islam cannot lay claim to the first 16 chapters of Genesis, then interject Ishmael into the 22nd Chapter of Genesis, while denying what unfolded through the rest of the book. Actually Islam was not the recognized religion that it is today, until the 7th Century, C.E. or A.D. The term Muslim means submitted to god, but their book of reference came long after the Hebrew

Scriptures and even the New Testament. So Islam has an interesting gap in their history as well as their belief system.

Claiming their "inheritance" as the children of Ishmael is, however; prophesied in Scripture, as early as the account of Hagar, Ishmael's mother. The G-d of Abraham did say he would bless them, but that was because of His covenant with Abraham, who also fathered Isaac, and the same Scriptures that Muslims use to claim their identity also says Isaac was the son of promise. To detour to a new book, while holding to the promised identity contained in Genesis, leaves much room for the Islamic detour away from YHWH. Technically, much of Christianity has used the New Testament to develop the same problem.

The foundation of many Christian denominations is the belief that the Messiah rendered G-d's Law, obsolete. If the man described in the accounts of the gospel did not uphold the Law of G-d, then he is not the Messiah sent by G-d. The gospel according to John tells us in the first chapter . . . The Word became flesh. G-d's Law is in His Word. Messiah is the Word in the flesh. To deny the Word, is to deny Messiah, and to deny obedience to the Word of G-d is to refuse to follow Messiah. To be "in Messiah" is to be obedient to G-d's Law.

Think not that I am come to destroy the law, or the prophets: I am not come to destroy, but to fulfil.
Matthew 5: 17

He that saith he abideth in him ought himself also so to walk, even as he walked.   *I John 2: 6*

And he was clothed with a vesture dipped in blood: and his name is called The Word of G-d.   *Revelation 19: 13*

Chapter 19

The Strong Delusion
is the
Delusion of Strength

There is an old saying that clearly describes what many are terming a conspiracy theory or political witch hunts of opposing prevailing parties. "The devil is in the details," and he is often referred to as a "shape shifter." Devil worship is not the only religion following the enemy. Scripture tells us self-exultation is actually the religion of the enemy . . . The best way to express self love is self indulgence and proud excess.

We have become a nation driven by money and material excess. The reward is supposed to be provision and the motivation and goal are presented to be combined; the children. While we are being told and led to believe we are doing what we're doing for the children, it is actually at the cost of our children. Our materialism has led us to spend less time with the children and simply indulge them in activities and possessions to prove our love. We begin the training early, in that all the hours spent away from them is actually something we are doing "for them."

I once heard a person say, "We have to choose to be deceived." We believe a lie because that's what we want to believe. Most of humanity that is aware of the Scriptural warning regarding the strong delusion, is simply counting on recognizing the sudden rise of a beastly government.

Growing up hearing about the pre-tribulation rapture and tribulation, in that order, I was being taught that the exit from the tribulation was the priority, placing the focus of the Second Coming on man rather than Messiah. I often wondered how all the world would agree upon a single religion, but then I read the book of the Revelation for myself. As it turns out, there is no mention of a rapture and the "bowing down" and worshiping was in reference to the entity that gave "everyone" what they wanted or thought they needed. According to the book of Daniel, the vision of the beasts was interpreted, by the angel, to be governments. "Bowing down," worship, and receiving a mark, refers to buying and selling, which of course simply states, the inhabitants of earth through this time will be horribly dependent in their materialism. All three religions espouse and claim supererogatory; in different areas, but excess, none the less.

When we think about it . . . isn't provision, prosperity, and power truly how our success, allegiance, and faith have become defined? Most Americans measure our existence by our possessions, thus Last Will and Testaments are common place. For most of the population, the standard of success is also measured by material possessions, and that has certainly spilled over into American Christianity. Many ministers espouse the teaching that a sign of the blessing of G-d is material possessions and a degree of wealth. Deuteronomy 28 is frequently quoted and does mention success and plenty, but in direct correlation to Torah obedience.

Islam, although supposedly anti-materialistic, mentions their god and he always sounds like a militant dictator offering women and pleasure as a reward. In seeing the lavish accommodations afforded their leaders and upper echelon, regardless of the poverty of the average citizen, the leadership lacks nothing materially.

Judaism is truly a religion unto it's own, and materialism is absolutely no stranger in those beliefs. Certainly, success is measured by a lifestyle of "comfortable." As Judaism has become based on Talmud interpretation over Torah, this religion has become more about what it is to "be Jewish." It is exclusive, and certainly much less aggressive in proselytizing than Christianity or Islam.

Christianity talks about G-d providing and Jesus interceding; yet dependence upon human intervention is common place.

Scripture gives more than one account in which the enemy of G-d's people has been allowed, even used by G-d to overpower His people in times of rebellion or to call His people to repentance and deliverance. Sometimes G-d has allowed His people to endure captivity, and other times He has responded to their cries of repentance with swift deliverance and victory. So far, we in this country, as a group, have seen neither to any degree, yet.

No one stole the freedom Adam and Eve enjoyed, they

willingly chose to give it up. A conspiracy theory that "they" are taking it all away from "us" is an interesting way to avoid the responsibility for what we are choosing, but it doesn't change the facts and it certainly won't change the outcome.

"They" or TPTB [the powers that be], in some circles referred to as "globalists," are more than likely driven by selfish desires and want of power, but "they" are also deceived. The powers that be may appear to have an agenda, but the reality is, their souls have been sold to the one with the agenda of evil and world domination. The enemy is not operating as merely a member of a conspiracy. The conspiracy theories are only decoys. There is no doubt, there is a "they" and there is no doubt there are globalists but they do not and will not have the ultimate power of the beastly government, they will only be "servant officials."

John wrote in his first letter that there were already many anti-Christs at that time. History, as well as current events, provides a view of spirits of anti-Christs in places of political power along the way. World wide, it is pretty much a rule of thumb that people bow down to their government or at least express some sort of allegiance or dependence upon their government, be it by fear, entitlement, or social tradition. We are already experiencing the mandate of some of those that have been deceived, and many that are deceiving.

And for this cause G-d shall send them strong delusion, that they should believe a lie:
II Thessalonians 2:11

Since this is a New Testament Scripture, it is not recognized in Judaism or Islam, but only in Christianity. The passage does, however; apply to all of humanity.

162

The strong delusion occurs in Christianity, world wide, when New Testament interpretation is made independently or in disregard of Old Testament teaching. The strong delusion has of course permeated Judaism in their rejection of Messiah. The strong delusion in Islam is abject delusion after Abraham, to Ishmael, to Mohammad 6 centuries after Messiah came, and then their attempt to connect and claim.

It's easy for many Christian Americans to see the error in Judaism and Islam, but Christian tradition is very intertwined in national observances and early Roman paganism. Just as in Islam, many Christian traditions and beliefs are not found in Scripture, but America's holidays, power, and commerce is based upon them.

The Arab nations possess the strong delusion that the world would be a better place if everyone behaved as they do. That obviously won't make the world better, for many reasons. Clearly these older leaders that are encouraging the young suicide bombers, know they would not be where they are, if they had followed their present teaching. The Arab nations only get along against someone else. If they truly were peaceable amidst themselves, the so called displaced Palestinians could have received the Sinai Peninsula, when Israel gave it up in the 70's.

Israel has the delusion that the government can operate outside of G-d's design and still be blessed by Him. Their right of return will only be blessed with the peace of G-d, when Israel is a Theocratic monarchy, and that time is yet to come.

One of America's delusions is exceedingly sad, in that we have so many copies of the Truth. The nations of Islam do not hate America because of Christianity, but rather because of our immoral, materialistic culture. License for a luxurious lifestyle, free of YHWH's Torah, after the death of Messiah, is pagan absurdity and render the practitioners of such, powerless.

Many errors have been made since the Nicene Creed was established, meaning more delusion. Most of European Christianity and certainly America's beliefs are based upon Roman Catholicism, either by continuation, or the protesting thereof, Protestantism. The inhabitants of these continents have taken their versions of Christianity around the world. If the fourth government in Daniel's vision was the Roman Empire, then clearly it has not yet been disestablished, but rather altered, expanded, evolved, and adapted.

The book of Daniel tells us that the fourth government will mix into a quasi newness, but will still only be a combination of the iron of the fourth power and clay, with clay being an obvious reference to humanity, and weaker than iron. It will be destroyed by the everlasting kingdom G-d has established.

America could be learning a lot from 3rd world countries. The strategy that we can expand our technological advancement, and through that technology we will eventually claim and declare victory, is a delusion. Creating chaos and crisis to bring order, is delusion. The one world order offering security, health, and protection is a delusion for all those that choose to believe a lie and to be deceived.

Our children learn political involvement and religious legacy from the adults in a society. The children in America are learning to hate and fight the very people they are told want to hate and fight them. That's not what Messiah taught.

News/Talk Radio eludes to the thought that one would obtain information, and yet the majority of that time is spent broadcasting ultra controversial, pseudo news, and or biased information, cloaked in editorialized arrogance by persons that refer to themselves as entertainers, not reporters. One of the sounds of "fiddling while Rome burns."

The connection between the ecumenical gospel that's been proclaimed for over 50 years in this country and the new faith based community initiatives is deception and a delusion that will ultimately lead it's followers into the idolatry of worship of the government.

Some people are actually looking for some new, never before imagined, anti-Christ creature with seven physical monstrous heads. Many of these same people, out of fear or allegiance, already revere their government and/or it's leadership. Perhaps they will see a seven headed monster, but the Apostle John wrote in his lifetime that there were already many anti-Christs. The book of Daniel clearly explained that the beasts he was shown were not literal images or beings, but symbolic of governments.

Would we really need an entire book of the Bible containing a warning to avoid worshiping a scary seven headed monster? Wouldn't the Scripture in Isaiah, "come let us reason together" indicate this reference might be symbolic?

We, humans, tend to focus on evil. We prefer to talk about something that offends us or frightens us, as to glorifying G-d and declaring HIS power. That fact can be seen from everything from abortion issues to terrorists. We like to focus on evil, and it certainly applies to end time events as we read about the last days. We theorize the recognition of the beast. We try to figure out what the mark will be. In all of this conjecture, we are giving the enemy credence and overlooking the awesome power of the One True G-d. The Bible is about G-d's love for His people and redemption. Even in the Scriptures regarding the Second Coming, it's not about the enemy or us, it's about seeing Messiah and G-d establishing His kingdom forever. Scripture tells us G-d will seal His people in their foreheads. The mark of the beast will only be a counterfeit copy of what G-d has done for His people. The seal of G-d is mentioned in the Revelation, several chapters before the mark of the beast.

Saying, Hurt not the earth, neither the sea, nor the trees, till we have sealed the servants of our G-d in their foreheads.

Revelation 7: 3

And the fourth kingdom shall be strong as iron: forasmuch as iron breaketh in pieces and subdueth all things: and as iron that breaketh all these, shall it break in pieces and bruise. And whereas thou sawest the feet and toes, part of potters' clay, and part of iron, the kingdom shall be divided; but there shall be in it of the strength of the iron, forasmuch as thou sawest the iron mixed with miry clay. And as the toes of the feet were part of iron, and part of clay, so the kingdom shall be partly strong, and partly broken. And whereas thou sawest iron mixed with miry clay, they shall mingle themselves with the seed of men: but they shall not cleave one to another, even as iron is not mixed with clay. And in the days of these kings shall the G-d of heaven set up a kingdom, which shall never be destroyed: and the kingdom shall not be left to other people, but it shall break in pieces and consume all these kingdoms, and it shall stand for ever. Forasmuch as thou sawest that the stone was cut out of the mountain without hands, and that it brake in pieces the iron, the brass, the clay, the silver, and the gold; the great G-d hath made known to the king what shall come to pass hereafter: and the dream is certain, and the interpretation thereof sure. *Daniel 2: 40-45*

And the heaven was open; and I saw a white horse, and he who was seated on it was named Certain and True; and he is judging and making war in righteousness. And his eyes are a flame of fire, and crowns are on his head; and he has a name in writing, of which no man has knowledge but himself. And he is clothed in a robe washed with blood: and his name is The Word of G-d. And the armies which are in heaven went after him on white horses, clothed in delicate linen, white and clean. And out of his mouth comes a sharp sword, with which he overcomes the nations: and he has rule over them with a rod of iron: and he is crushing with his feet the grapes of the strong wrath of G-d the Ruler of all . . .And I saw the beast, and the kings of the earth, and their armies, come together to make war against him who was seated on the horse and against his army.

Revelation 19: 11- 15, 19

Chapter 20

The False Foundation

The doctrine of the Nicolaitans, those warned against and admonished by John the Revelator, held the foundational teaching of those that were later gathered by Constantine as the Fathers of the First Council of Nicaea. The Nicene Creed is the formal doctrine produced by Constantine's religious leaders in his attempt to separate belief in Messiah from Judaism and bring the "new" religion under his empire. The teaching of the Nicolaitans was that of congregational subservience both in religion and government. The citizens were 'ordained' to be servants to the leaders. This teaching was a dangerous heretical combination of claiming the authority of the Apostles, while teaching their own brand of righteousness and false doctrine of religious hierarchy, outside of the standard of YHWH's statutes. As the Nicolaitans continued in their infiltration of the 1st Century assembly of believers, it became the perfect basis for a political leader to exercise authority without accountability, and religious leaders to develop their self-sanctioned office of unquestionable dominance.

Until the reign of Constantine there was no New Testament, so the reference that Paul made in one of his letters to Timothy about rightly dividing the Word of Truth, had absolutely no reference to any Scripture except the Hebrew Scripture, also called the Old Testament. His statement was in regard to interpretation of what was referred to as Oral Torah, explained in the Talmud, which was taught by Jewish leaders at the time. Much of the population was not highly educated. In the first Century following Messiah's life, death and resurrection, the Apostles were clearly Jewish and the Gentile believers were added to that number. G-d's definition of the house of Israel and man's definition vary in some dramatic ways, but G-d's plan of completion for His people and prophetic fulfillment in the life and death of Messiah did not render any of His Word obsolete.

His statutes are still intact and quite applicable today, on an individual basis. The better covenant referred to in the book of Hebrews is the covenant of the perfect blood of Messiah, rather than that of bulls and rams. The better covenant is one of deletion of sin, rather than covering it. Messiah, by the grace of G-d, was the final sacrifice, therefore eliminating the need for ongoing, annual animal sacrifice. His death, however; did not redefine sin, nor did it remove the obligation of obedience. Sin is still defined in Torah, as is obedience, and any religious tradition or interpretation that teaches otherwise is not teaching according to the Word of G-d, or as stated in Paul's letter, not "rightly dividing the Word of Truth."

The Nicene Creed brought about a stark division between those who were following Messiah and those who were following the misinterpretation of Saul of Tarshish, also known as the Apostle Paul. If Paul taught against Torah, he was the imposter spoken of in Deuteronomy 13: 6-10. If Paul taught against the self-righteousness espoused by Talmudic Pharisees and Sanhedrin, rejected the Talmud and remained Torah observant while proclaiming Messiah, then he was in fact to be counted among the Apostles.

I, personally believe that Paul was an Apostle, and what makes his ministry so full of promise to us today is not the unaffixed interpretation of his epistles, but rather the documentation in the book of Acts. The book of Acts details the wonders that G-d manifested through the life of Paul. Even though he did not walk with Y'hshuwah through Y'hshuwah's time on earth, and by Paul's own confession, prior to his conversion, he had actually persecuted those that did follow Messiah. The book of Acts also clearly reveals that Paul continued to observe the Holy Days and in
I Corinthians encouraged those converts in that very prosperous city of Corinth, to do the same.

The fact that Paul received this presence of the Spirit and power of G-d in his life, should be a source of encouragement to all of us today. The details recorded by Luke in the book of Acts, indicate that the promise and presence and power of the Holy G-d of Scripture, is still available to those that would also abandon their own definition of righteousness espoused by false religious teachings. To repent from one's own excuses and definition of right and wrong, is fundamental in seeking G-d and receiving His forgiveness. Frequently, the letters of Paul are not interpreted to that cause, but rather interpreted to reinforce and justify the very thing that caused Paul to refer to himself as chief among sinners.

Paul was religiously a devout man and by Talmud's definition, righteous. The Pharisees had done what so many still do today. The human interpretation of G-d's Word was now the core of their religion, rather than G-d, Himself. The actual Word of G-d was now a point of open debate, while the Talmudic teachings had become 'law.'

Constantine's First Council of Nicaea produced the Nicene Creed, and with it some profound religious traditions were formed that still stand today. The Trinity was declared. Passover and the Crucifixion were carefully and officially separated by the Council, to not be observed in concurrence or in accordance with the historical timing, outlined in Scripture. The observance of the Crucifixion was then designated to be an observance of the resurrection and to follow the vernal equinox.

The fundamental flaw with the trinity theory can be found in the New Testament in many places. The New Testament literally disproves the trinity. The trinity idea came from a Roman belief system involving mythological gods referred to in the book of Acts.

In the book of James we are told, *"G-d cannot be tempted"* . . . Y'hshuwah was tempted

We are promised to be *"joint heirs with Messiah"* The trinity teaching defines Messiah to be G-d, so joint with Messiah, would indicate believers become gods.

John 3: 16 refers to *G-d's Son.* Children are not the same as parents and children are never equal with parents, as defined in Scripture.

Hebrews tells us *Y'hshuwah sits at the right hand of Majesty.*

The Revelation clearly speaks separately of G-d and Messiah, who is the Lamb.

172

As a political leader that "found" religion, Constantine made some matters of his belief, points of civil law. Sunday was designated to be a day of rest or worship. It was not religious doctrine but civil law. Man's law officially overrode Torah in the name of Christian leadership, while carefully maintaining the separation of the true church and state. Constantine claimed the authority to draw the line between the religious establishment of the Nicenes and the politically incorrect Nazarenes. Approximately 250 years before Constantine ruled, Scripture reveals to us in the second chapter of the Revelation, G-d had already clearly drawn that line.

Unfortunately much of Christianity has become Christology. There is nothing wrong with learning about the attributes and accomplishments of Messiah. We are called to know him and learn of him. Along with bringing redemption, he set the standard for us to live, which he said to emulate. He did not come to provide excuses for imperfection, nor to establish a religion apart from the Holy Scripture, known as the Old Testament, nor did he come to nullify the Law of G-d. He came to be a ransom for many and he came to bring us to the Father. A relationship is not knowledge about, but rather, to know and to know personally. In Matthew 11: 29, Messiah invites us to *"Take my yoke upon you, and learn of me . . ."*

Paul later warned Timothy of the coming apostasy that could easily and deceptively make it's way into the various branches of theology and Christology, that were yet to come. Paul's last letter to the young pastor offered encouragement and insight, while also containing ominous prophesy.

This know also, that in the last days perilous times shall come. For men shall be lovers of their own selves . . . Having a form of godliness, but denying the power

thereof: from such turn away . . . Ever learning, and
never able to come to the knowledge of the truth.
II Timothy 3: 1, 5, 7

It's easy to see the material wealth in Vatican City, but much of the non-denominational independent churches have in effect developed their own little Rome with little or no accountability. The prosperity preachers are basically independent Popes. The prosperity of these independent leaders does not come in the way they teach their followers, rather I should say, their follower's prosperity does not come in the same way as the leaders. The leaders receive their prosperity by the ignorant generosity of their followers.

Just as the Nicolaitans taught nearly twenty centuries ago, many people today believe they are to take care and provide for their leaders, to serve; if you will. We know everyone cannot make an above comfortable living by 'passing the plate' or these days, the buckets, but is this method any better than the one warned about in the message to the church at Pergamos?

But my G-d shall supply all your need according to His
riches in glory by Messiah Y'hshuwah.
Philippians 4: 19

Actually, the hierarchy, multi-pastor inner circle establishment of the mega-church bears a striking resemblance to the governmental workings of the Roman Catholic Church, with the exception of individual independence. And we certainly cannot omit the entourage of ushers and body guards. Each mega-organization has it's own leader of near inaccessibility, with which the humble members hope to gain audience.

Those that follow the present mainstream interpretation of the New Testament, specifically in regard to the interpretation of Paul's writings are following the teachings of the Nicene Council and are not following the Messiah, who lived by Torah, perfectly. The widely accepted current interpretation of Scripture, in many ways is simply wrong. The concept that the New Testament eliminated the values and standards of the Old Testament is religious insanity at best and blasphemy at worst. The truth has been cast aside to embrace heretical tradition that infiltrated the early church and later was officially established and documented in the third century A.D. or C.E. Scripture is inerrant, humanity is not. People and interpretation are quite frequently in error.

Through this particular political/religious establishment, the prophecy of Daniel 7: 25 came to pass and continues to stand to this day. The term A.D., literally divides the time. Some use the letters C.E., rather than A.D. C.E. acknowledges the continuity of time, and depending upon the perspective, C.E. represents either Common Era or Christian Era.

Pope Gregory of the Roman Catholic Church is the man for whom the calendar of dividing of time is named. The Gregorian calendar is the one declared to replace the Julian calendar in the late 1500's, but was not officially recognized by England and the properties for nearly two more centuries, with a few exceptions even as late as the early 20th Century. Until the late 1700's, which just happens to coincide with the founding of America, the calendars varied, according to cultures, with the Julian calendar of the ruling Roman Empire, being the most prevalent. The Hebrew calendar has remained consistent and continuous through the centuries. Scripture is very clear in regard to the way G-d has established the months and seasons. Although much religious tradition and ritual has been added to many observances, the Hebrew calendar has maintained the established times and days in accordance with the Laws of G-d.

Pope Gregory, by giving his approval, gave religious credence to the calendar designed by Aloysius Lilius. The Italian doctor, Lilius, was also an astronomer, philosopher and chronologist who devised what is now recognized the world over as the Gregorian calendar. Just in this one example, the evidence is offered for a combined power of religion, government, and science to mandate prophesied change, affecting the entire world to function globally in synchronization. Many of the months on the Gregorian calendar are named for false Roman deity, as are the days of the week, yet it bears the name of the Pope. Lilius had such lasting influence, even the modern technology of computer science recognizes him with the Lilian date. The Lilian date is the number of days since the formal adoption of the Gregorian Calendar, October 14, 1582.
October 15, 1582 is Lilian day 1.

And he shall speak great words against the most High, and shall wear out the saints of the most High, and think to change times and laws: and they shall be given into his hand until a time and times and the dividing of time.   *Daniel 7: 25*

So hast thou also them that hold the doctrine of the Nicolaitanes, which thing I hate.
                                 Revelation 2: 15

Chapter 21

Self-ism, The Trinity of Me, Myself, and I

The religion of self worship. Although it has many euphemisms and rather than just use the term selfish, I'll refer to it as self-ism. The three major world religions already openly acknowledge that secularism is a false religion, and when the term, human is added, the focus becomes all about the ME. Secular humanism is comfortable with the concept and priority of self importance. There is self-actualization, self-esteem, self-worth, self- etc. While the big three religions have their own agenda of self-ism.

Religious self-ism is a bit more obscure than secular humanism; obscure to the point of abject camouflaged denial.

The Muslims envision their domination and their paradise of 70 virgins, which is obviously all about self and pleasure. The majority of mainstream Christians want a pastor that makes them feel good, promises prosperity in this life, and reigning power in the next. Again the priority of self. And the Jews have been asking for years in the political arena, "Is it good for the Jews?" These concepts are held by the devout members of these religions. An obvious priority of the collective 'self.' Self-ism doesn't seem so selfish, when it's a group concern.

The basic understanding of the religion of self is that it can exist quite comfortably within any of the three main religions as well as all the others, even be interwoven into the tenets of the faith. The term secular is usually applied as an adjective for an individual less dedicated in Islam and Judaism that manages their religion around their priorities, i.e., secular Muslim or secular Jew. Christianity tends to use the terms, worldly or backslidden, as their adjectives for those lacking piety, which replace the antiquated term; carnal.

Basically we have the center of our concerns and focus to be ourselves, and in that we need a government that will protect and take care of us. We need a religious organization that meets our needs and encourages us. We need healthcare that will not leave us waiting, wanting, or entering eternity, but will see to us, post haste. We need legislation that will cause the world to accommodate us in our special victimization or morality. We need the information biased to accommodate our itching ears. We need to have less stress and more stuff. We need the world to revolve around us . . . And we need, for the rest of the world to understand that is the proper order in the new world order.

All of these things take money, and Scripture tells us the love of money is the root of all the evil. Even though there is an old cliché that says "money can't buy happiness" most people seem assured that it will make misery much more comfortable. The one world religion is self.

It really does just boil down to self. Is it good for me? Self-esteem, self-accomplished, self-control. Scripture mentions self-control, but rather than controlling our desires, the context which is most embraced, is that all the control should belong to me, or those whose thinking most aligns with mine. Clearly, my decisions and best interest are what is needed for all of us. And the interesting fact is, we can justify what ever we want, rendering us in the wonderfully euphoric state of self-satisfaction in our own self-righteousness. We all know, regardless of religion or lack thereof, that our god wants what's best for us, and most believe what we want is what's best for us!

We have listened to so many promises for so many years that we really don't realize it is selfish ambition that shapes our decisions. It is actually part of our culture at this point. What is best for me and mine is foundational to every decision we make. We are taught that a good income is the way to provide for everything from the needs of our children to our needs in old age. And we are taught the road to a good income is a good education, and a good education teaches us we need self-esteem for self-actualization to be self-accomplished. The education system is teaching that humanism is the way to wealth and happiness. And the church teaches that G-d is the way to peace and prosperity. Undoubtedly, there is some truth to both of these teachings, but the essence and error of both teachings focuses on the end results for self, with the emphasis on riches.

Very few would even consider arguing that one of the purposes of the education system should be, to reach the children and make them feel good about who they are, which is self-esteem. And of course we know that the education system provides the necessary tools to earn a living. The level of income to which one aspires is pretty much proportionate to the level of education to which one acquires.

Y'hshuwah said He is the Way, the Truth, and the Life and that He came to bring us to the Father. We must deny ourselves and follow Him. Deny self? Who teaches that, these days? Just what does that mean? Even most of the so called religious holidays are not observed as holy days. Most holidays are a commercialized event and in my observation, a contraction of the words holy and day, while maintaining "I" as the center; hol - I - day.

It's easy for "I" or self to become the focus of our beliefs, because we start most statements of faith with the word, I. I believe or I know . . . I can hear something and believe it, I can experience something and know it, but when I read something in Scripture, I can believe it and know it. I know and I believe G-d has a purpose for every life He creates and I know He wants to bless His people. Scripture tells us that. Unfortunately the trendy popular belief and expectation of how He chooses to bless, is now according to human interpretation.

Scripture also tells us, G-d's ways are not our ways. The 121 Psalm says, G-d neither slumbers nor sleeps, but I simply do not believe that G-d stays up nights planning the next day to revolve around me and to make everything go my way. Scripture warns in many places about false teachers, false prophets, and those who speak what the people want to hear. I remember some pretty dark times in my life in the past, and I can honestly say, if I hadn't come to know G-d and know His voice, I would certainly be drawn to the self-focused doctrine. I'm a goal oriented person, so a motivational speaker would truly reach me. We all appreciate inspiration, especially when it's something we want to hear and makes us feel good.

Some people feel it's a good preacher when they hear about sin and condemnation. Others feel good, hearing about G-d's forgiveness, still others appreciate knowing G-d is love. Actually, all those facets of spiritual teaching are true, but the one thing that we all need to face, is worship is not supposed to be about us, regardless of how we feel or how we want to feel. Worship is about G-d. Y'hshuwah's parting instructions to his disciples, are ***"Go ye therefore, and teach all nations, baptizing them in the Name of the Father, and of the Son, and of the Holy Ghost: Teaching them to observe all things whatsoever I have commanded you: and, lo, I am with you alway, even unto the end of the world. Amen."***
Matthew 28: 19-20

Not a word about motivational inspiration. Nothing about an uplifting message, so people feel better. He had already given them the power to heal! When various members of this trendy teaching start telling me about Holy Ghost goose bumps and spirit filled anointed teaching, or mega-dollar blessings, for the most part, I just have to get away. Acts 1:8 tells us specifically what the gift of the Holy Spirit will produce and further details are contained in I Corinthians 12. It simply never mentions goose bumps, heat spots, outlandish behavior, or self satisfaction. If worship is about how it makes "us" feel, then just whom has received the focus of our worship? Whether it's religion or politics, we have a tendency to appreciate the demagogue that promotes our own ideology or agrees with our first priority. For many, that priority; is self.

And he said to them all, If any man will come after me, let him deny himself, and take up his cross daily, and follow me.

Luke 9: 23

And his power shall be mighty, but not by his own power: and he shall destroy wonderfully, and shall prosper, and practice, and shall destroy the mighty and the holy people. And through his policy also he shall cause craft to prosper in his hand; and he shall magnify himself in his heart, and by peace shall destroy many: he shall also stand up against the Prince of princes; but he shall be broken without hand.

Daniel 8: 24, 25

And they overcame him by the blood of the Lamb, and by the word of their testimony; and they loved not their lives unto the death.

Revelation 12: 11

Chapter 22

We Live What We Believe

Living large, is precisely what we, as a society, believe. I once received a note written on the back of a "script" for a youth outreach program of a Mega-church. I'm so glad that I actually knew G-d, rather than associate HIM with that scripted message, I read. I wasn't even remotely interested in what was being introduced or promoted, and I was abhorred at the programming of that youth department. Scripture certainly doesn't mince words as to G-d's view of misleading children. This script to which I refer was one of an older youth group, but obviously these young people were conditioned and encouraged to believe what they were being led to do and say.

The other approach that I find alarming is

predominantly done by the churches that want to be Mega-churches, but just haven't quite found the spark to do so. A pastor of one of those organizations, once explained to me that they used all the hype, promises, and gifts as "bait" and once the people come in, they share the gospel. He said it was a particularly beneficial youth outreach tool. I could easily see for myself, his term "bait" was his euphemism for idolatry. Y'hshuwah didn't use bait, he didn't need bait. He met needs. Which brings us to the next interesting updated interpretation.

In the "spirit of meeting needs," worship is now designed to accommodate the worshipper. It's "user friendly," so to speak. Auditoriums have replaced sanctuaries. High tech worship, pumps up the volume. Supersize the 7/11 songs on the overhead. 7/11 songs contain about 11 words and they are repeated 7 times, give or take a time or twenty. I remember, as a teen, when the religious leaders of America realized music affected the listener. Of course, that was a warning against rock and roll, at the time. Now there are Christian rock and roll concerts, in the churches! So, when the music is loud, repetitive, and consuming, the crowd becomes amenable. And without a doubt, the mega church has found the "amen" in amenable. Scripture tells us that David played music to soothe Saul. Sadly, today, many do not know the difference between soothing and mesmerizing, much less praise or programming. The "praise and worship" portion of the service continues until the "attitude and atmosphere" of worship has been established a.k.a. getting ready to pass the plate. Although, it's no longer plates that are passed.

I've noticed the offerings appeared to be collected in something that resembles KFC Chicken buckets or popcorn tubs at the movies. A subtle correlation with being satisfied and entertained? Y'hshuwah is recorded in

Mark's account of the gospel as clearly giving the instruction to pass <u>no</u> vessels in the temple.

And they come to Jerusalem: and Y'hshuwah went into the temple, and began to cast out them that sold and bought in the temple, and overthrew the tables of the moneychangers, and the seats of them that sold doves; And would not suffer that any man should carry any vessel through the temple. And he taught, saying unto them, Is it not written, My house shall be called of all nations the house of prayer? but ye have made it a den of thieves.

Mark 11: 15-17

As the worshipper is accommodated, the message or mantra is clearly and repetitively taught that G-d wants to bless them. Scripture does teach that G-d takes care of HIS people, blesses us, meets our needs and answers our prayers. So Name it and Claim it, Blab it and Grab it, and read the latest book . . . If the pastor has written one, all the better. All the latest books are usually available right outside the "auditorium," there at the money changers on your way out, a.k.a. book store, by the "Prayer café" or "Fellowship coffee house" down the hall from the "Upper Room" and "Purpose filled Video Game Room." I actually saw, with my own eyes, a sign board at one of those mega-church complexes, giving the hours when the "prophet is in" to make an appointment and see what is in store for your life, presented as, what G-d has planned for your life . . .

Ah, the atmosphere of accommodated worshippers. Just where do we find all these user-friendly worship techniques in the Instruction Manual?

I've always felt that attending the mega-church is a lot like going to the circus or the coliseum, both of which enkindle absolutely no comfort in my soul. Although I've never attended an event in a coliseum, I have visited the ruins in Greece and read about the events. I have, however; been to both the Mega-church and the circus, relatively the same number of times, and they have just always evoked the same dreaded excitement, an agitation of sorts. I was one of the few kids that did not enjoy the circus and as an adult, I feel the same way about the Mega-church. As a matter of fact, I always hear the sound of the Calliope when I enter the auditorium of the Mega-Church. Whether it's little cars full of clowns or Harleys down the aisle, there's quite a show in town under the big top! I'm guessing that's just one of the many sounds that drowns out the playing of the fiddle as Rome burns, still.

When I was a young person, the conservative religious organizations at the time taught if there was so much as half an ounce of untruth in a teaching, it was unsound as doctrine. Now, a half an ounce of truth is all that's needed in the religious rhetoric and it's time to start a building fund and TV ministry. The Mega-church has super-sized, self-defined sanctimony. I just can't help but wonder how many people come away thinking the Mega-church experience is a reflection of the G-d of Scripture? Apparently the number is quite large and growing.

Whether it's Wal-Mart, McDonald's, or the Mega-Church, we are consumers. And just like the options at a fast food drive through, we want instant, we want extra large, and we want what we want, now. If the twelve sons of one man could have established such a profound impact on the world as Israel has; and if twelve men following the Messiah had such an effect on the world that every government and religion known, tried and couldn't stop them, why have Evangelical crusades and the Mega Church resulted in so little? Oh, I know, everyone that attends week after week, "feels" so profoundly changed, but the twelve men of whom I refer, profoundly changed the world.

I wonder . . .

Since we are hearing about living large, rather than "take up they cross and follow Me" . . . Even the word, Epiphany, has been redefined, What once meant, Messiah revealed, has become merely an idea, frequently pertaining to marketing. Are the young people and those seeking help or hope, being persuaded that blessings can be bought for a donation?

I have actually seen someone figure the amount they owed or "needed" to determine the size of the offering check being written. I'm about to share 2 personal experiences regarding the 100 fold heresy teaching.

The first situation was truly earth shattering, as I was still attempting to "be in one accord" but I've also come to understand we are not called to fellowship with the servants of Baal. Materialism is certainly a false god. I was answering a prayer line for the local TV programming and had been for some time, back in the 90s. The "Collect-A-Thon" began, which I was not thrilled to be working, anyway, but the confusion caused me to draw a line that I will not cross. People were calling in with pledges for the organization, when a person asked me to help them figure their donation. I had no idea what they were talking about.

I went and turned on the TV, and sure enough, the preacher was explaining that G-d wanted HIS people to be debt free. I certainly couldn't argue with that. Then I was shocked at the next step in this teaching. They simply needed to "tithe" on their debt and HE would "bless them" with the amount due. Scripture teaches we are to tithe on our income, the first fruits, not our debt. When I mentioned that to the station manager, I was informed that I had a decision to make, but questioning Rev. So and So, was out of the question. So it was, I was no longer needed to answer the prayer line.

The last incident was perhaps, a bit more humorous. I met a minister at a conference who was talking to me about his big outreach ministry. He had a vision for a program, etc. that would cost $10,000 a month and he wanted to know if I wanted to donate and "reap" the 100 fold increase harvest to finance my ministry. I told him, I'd be happy to help him out. I had a ministry that only cost $100 a month. He could donate a hundred dollars to my ministry and the 100 fold increase would cover the cost of his $10,000 vision. And so, he walked away.

Now, mind you these prosperity teachers aren't telling people to kill others for a reward or anything like that. It's more a matter of teaching materialism to be spiritual. I call it the Laodicean doctrine. The proclamation is made, in the name of Jesus, that serving G-d and mammon are compatible for a lifestyle. Actually the teaching sounds to be more a matter of "Serve G-d, He's serving up mammon."

So then because thou art lukewarm, and neither cold nor hot, I will spue thee out of my mouth. Because thou sayest, I am rich, and increased with goods, and have need of nothing; and knowest not that thou art wretched, and miserable, and poor, and blind, and naked: I counsel thee to buy of me gold tried in the fire, that thou mayest be rich; and white raiment, that thou mayest be clothed, and that the shame of thy nakedness do not appear; and anoint thine eyes with eyesalve, that thou mayest see.   *Revelation 3: 16-18*

Chapter 23

Political Correctness

I remember reading an article several years ago, that addressed whether PC would ever take root. Would PC catch on? The writer of the article didn't think it could come to be in our society. I think back and realize, the introduction of acronyms in articles. Now, some fifteen years later, do the initials PC officially refer to political correctness or personal computer? Regardless, the subject at hand is political correctness; and the times, they have changed. What is it to be politically correct and just who, with devout beliefs, is actually religiously tolerant?

Through the years, it has been revealed in many ways, that G-d truly prepares us for the call HE has placed upon our lives. I was given the prophet's preview in the 60's of political correctness, long before the term was in existence. I have a perfect example that has nothing to do with difference of race or economics, but a required sameness that served as my prelude to political correctness. My mother held my sister and I into the framework of sameness and equality, and defined the term fair, as she determined it to be. We're three years apart, yet we were dressed alike, treated the same and we never fought, as in a false standard of tolerance. I'm sure we had things to fight about, we were kids, after all; but we were not allowed to fight. It was simply and rigidly forbidden. My mother has actually informed my grandchildren when they disagree or bicker that she didn't allow their G-ma to fight with her sister. Aalthough she is far from being a proponent of political correctness, she defined it long before the trend.

My sister and I actually blazed the trail of political correctness without the benefit of taking refuge behind the closed door of the privacy of home. We weren't just politically correct publicly, we lived it. Until I was 10, we even shared the same room. There was absolutely no place to let down the facade of the political correctness that was required with equality and sameness, even though we were different in every way. Actually, from my perspective, the differences were marked, as I was the "overly dramatic," fat one who was three years older. Now, did that make us more tolerant of each other? Take a guess. I did, however; gain great insight of what was to come, in regard to "political correctness." It had to look the same, sound tolerant, and meet the expectation of the rule of law, but it did not reflect our hearts.

With the insight to political correctness, I also learned first hand, that life in fact, is not fair! And we still have this in America today, as it relates racially, economically, religiously and politically. To be perfectly correct in our correctness, people are different and tolerance does not mean sameness.

A brief definition of the word tolerance from WordWeb is as follows: 1. A disposition to allow freedom of choice and behavior   2. Willingness to recognize and respect the beliefs or practices of others.

Tolerance as defined by usage in society today, has been inverted and turned inside out, until; to be politically correct, is to have no individuality at all. In the name of tolerance, social pressure and legislation is enacted to accommodate a loud individual or minority that chooses to be offended. The tolerance defined by political correctness is actually obliterating some of the amendments in the Bill of Rights.

The pledge of allegiance has become an interesting test of tolerance. Since I do not pledge faith in anything or anyone but G-d, I consider pledging to a symbol to be idolatry. I do not, however; believe that my views should be forced upon the majority, or even upon others that may decline to pledge for different reasons. The way I truly understand the symbolism of our flag is the representation of freedom, and that includes the freedom to, or not to pledge allegiance to a symbol. I do not need to debate the "under G-d" portion of the pledge, the entire earth is beneath G-d, and that line wasn't added until the 50's anyway. It's simply a moot point, according to my beliefs, not a reason to demand political correctness of everyone else.

The antonym of tolerance, is intolerance, and by definition intolerance is the unwillingness to recognize or accept different beliefs and views. To impose the sentence of political correctness in our society is to validate, authorize, and reward, intolerance.

I've listened in my lifetime as something very significant has changed. At one time, people prayed for their needs and spoke prayers for the needs of others, now I have heard political leaders speak of "our blessings are with them . . ." We hear frequently the words, "our thoughts and prayers are with . . ." I've now heard "our thoughts are with . . ." and, of course, even though human blessings and thoughts have never equated to the power of G-d, the noticeable phrase that will be attributed to the New Age movement is the phraseology "we'll focus our intentions . . ."

Prayer is not intentions. We as humans, truly do not possess the power to bless anyone, although we can be used of G-d, to do so. Actually prayer in and of itself has no power. The power lies in whom or Whom one is praying to. If the prayer reaches the ear of the G-d of the universe, therein lies the power and HIS answer is unmistakable in manifestation.

This time, the Great Babylon will rise up from within, just as the Pharisees did, over 2000 years ago. When I served as police chaplain, I heard the beginning rumblings that began as supposed consideration for all faiths, the "request" to use euphemisms for G-d. Well, the reality is, G-d is not the Name of the Supreme Creator. And, of course, the name of Jesus became an issue, instantly. I was blessed to already be tagged, politically and religiously incorrect, so I was operating outside of the paradigm of mainstream, as it was. Many religious folk in this country, pride themselves in being politically incorrect. If I understand their doctrine correctly, it's a goal of their spirituality, a sign of piety. But to be religiously incorrect amidst mainstream religion and law enforcement makes a person as unpopular today, as it did in Jerusalem about 2000 years ago.

In order for the International Conference of Police Chaplains to live up to their own logic and PR, they had to accommodate my refusal to be politically correct. I reminded them that the word, god, was simply a reference to an object or person of worship.

G-d, Himself referred to other gods, so I was happy to not use the word god, I would be willing to refer to HIM by HIS title or specific name. When inquiry was made regarding my use of the name of Jesus, I said, I called him by his Hebrew name, Y'hshuwah. Again, I didn't argue their own rules, because they made no sense. It, of course, finally came down to the fact that other world religions do not veil their beliefs, terms, and convictions, so why would anyone that is serving the One True Living G-d, who is YHWH? His servants have never been politically or religiously correct, yet they never had to aim at incorrectness, either. They simply served Him according to His Word and it's still the same today . . . Nothing new under the sun.

Then Peter and the other apostles answered and said, We ought to obey G-d rather than men.
Acts 5: 29

The old cliché for political correctness is a reference about a "squeaky wheel getting the oil . . ."
Speaking of oil. Much of the pressure to be politically correct in American society is to avoid religiously offending our "suppliers."

If it be so, our G-d whom we serve is able to deliver us from the burning fiery furnace, and HE will deliver us out of thine hand, O king. But if not, be it known unto thee, O king, that we will not serve thy gods, nor worship the golden image which thou hast set up.
Daniel 3: 17, 18

I know thy works and where thou dwellest, even where Satan's seat is: and thou holdest fast my name, and hast not denied my faith, even in those days wherein Antipas was my faithful martyr, who was slain among you, where Satan dwelleth.

Revelation 2: 13

Chapter 24

Back to Babel

Political correctness is not entering our society without purpose. Forced redefinition and expected behavior is just the foundation. As the powers unite into one, a common language will be needed and has already been introduced. The term, Technolese, is my personal choice, along with a few forum writers and bloggers, to describe this new "language" of the 21st Century. Technolese, as I understand it, is a sort of spoken or recognized short hand that can be comprised of acronyms and initials or words designated for technical description. Acronyms and initials will be the language of technocracy, spoken fluently by the technocrats, and already infiltrating many areas of society. Acronyms and Initials are the Code of the Technocratic Power. These overlapping references are the encryption of the New World Order. The Initials are the monogram of monocracy.

WARNING: This chapter will live up to the title! These various details are provided only as a reference, as the list continues to grow . . . Milestones, if you will, of this journey to the new world order.

There are three arenas that primarily use initials and acronyms, but that number will increase with time, globalization, and subjugation. For right now, the three primary groups that are actively encrypting their language and references are technology, governmental bureaucracy, and health care, but the expansion into other areas and by the rest of society is happening at a rapid rate.

What do these various groupings of letters mean?

I entered just the word "acronyms" in a Google Search and discovered there were over 25 million hits on that word, so obviously it isn't just me, taking note of this new "language." Upon further reading, I found compilations of acronyms, with the lists ranging in number from 410,000 to 4 million. Already, there are millions of acronyms on record, although some very obscure; used in some area of research, data, or reference expertise. Considering the number of acronyms and initials, it's hard to believe so many have more than one meaning, but then again, that accounts for the astronomical list and apparently accumulating collection.

Actually, the use of initials and acronyms can mean a number of things. Try entering any small group of letters into a Google Search and just see the number of possibilities. I visited a website just this morning called acronymfinder.com that boasted a list containing over 4 million acronyms and initial references. This sentence was written at least three months before this book was published, so I would imagine the number is even greater, by now. I didn't take the time to actually confirm or verify that number, but I did peruse the sight and was sufficiently overwhelmed to realize that this is by now, an actual language in it's own right.

Here are just a few examples of already recognized and generally understood terms of technolese, and some that may be misunderstood later. The two letters; GM can refer to General Motors or Genetically Modified. If it's a car, we associate GM with a C and it's a Chevrolet, Buick, Pontiac or Cadillac, or a truck. According to headlines, I'm not sure how long GM will continue to be letters that represent a company that makes vehicles. When we hear genetically modified, frequently an O, for organism, follows the GM. GMO is the coded message to inform us our food has been tampered with. We may choose to not heed the warning, but that is the message. GMO is biotechnology that usually indicates the DNA of our edible vegetation has been crossed with something of a different organic nature, and the added DNA is frequently from some sort of living organism with the hybrid result of what is known as Transgenic. When I'm driving something from GM, I know what I'm dealing with. When I'm eating something labeled GM, I may in fact be eating grain that has the DNA for a digestive system of it's own.

How long has GE stood for General Electric in our society? We'll see those two letters with an altogether new meaning as life continues and technology advances. GE is now used to reference genetic engineering.

DoC is a reference to two entirely different departments, at least for the time being, they are different and separate. It refers to either Department of Commerce or Department of Corrections. We received a questionnaire from our "representative" asking our view of various options regarding prison overcrowding and crime and punishment. There was a question addressing work release programs and another one regarding chain gangs. Perhaps, although this thought is pure speculation at this point, somewhere the plan exists to have at least one member of the global community maintain the Department of Commerce with a workforce from the Department of Corrections.

Whenever the term global is used, the United Nations naturally comes to mind. This organization is expansive and must be recognized as a major component of the globalization process. I try to stay aware of what all these various initials represent, but I have come to realize, that also, is part of the plan. It has become my pet peeve, hinging upon obsession, to observe and attempt to understand as the media and politicians toss around a few initials in most every speech and article. To have a global government, or One World Order, a centralized method of communication is necessary. This centralized communication or language, if you will, is already present in everything from political speeches, to science and medicine, to text messaging at the local high school.

The acronyms associated with the United Nations are numerous and known in many languages. Most terms that begin with UN____, are generally recognized to be associated with the United Nations, such as UNICEF and UNESCO, for example.   In researching this chapter, I visited the membership page of the UN. http://www.un.org/members/   On this page are links and lists, but in clear, large lettering this is the statement on the page:

"Membership in the United Nations is open to all other peace-loving states which accept the obligations contained in the present Charter and, in the judgment of the Organization, are able and willing to carry out these obligations.

The admission of any such state to membership in the United Nations will be effected by a decision of the

General Assembly upon the recommendation of the Security Council."

When I read that all members are referred to and recognized as states, I decided to check the membership. Imagine my surprise to discover many of the countries that we are now battling or calling for sanctions to be instituted, are also "peace-loving states" of this same organization.

I've heard for years that the UN is the one world government. I think it's a sort of decoy for our own justification, or perhaps one arm of power or a part of the framework for the horrifically beastly government. The UN appears to be the record keeping branch of united world powers, and I think will possibly serve to be the "stenographer" that serves the court of the one world government. Maybe I just don't want to think of the fact that if the UN is the actual government of the beast, my nation has already pledged allegiance and actually hosts the headquarters.

The UN is not an entity unto itself, rather, it is comprised of countries that have agreed to call themselves "states" to participate and believe in the organization they have created. The UN is made up of its members, therefore it is not a separate ominous entity, but is merely host to those with likeminded goals. Considering the fact that the United States and Iran became members of this organization on the same day, I think it's safe to say unanimity is not instantly on the horizon.

I do think the UN is a fundamental instrument of power for those that hold the vision of the New World Order. When the global government is finally in place, all presently recognized sovereign nations will take their dutiful and authoritative position as bureaucracies in this evil composite of a government. According to the book of Daniel, this government will only be broken by the stone not cut out by human hands, which I believe to be the same stone referred to in Isaiah and Peter, the cornerstone; who is Messiah.

We have been trained in a rather Pavlovian manner to recognize and respond "accordingly" and "appropriately" to the various initials. Initials signify authority or respectability, and often even intimidating dominance. IRS means accountability regarding the tax system, for the citizens. To be approached or sought by the FBI means legal matters of national importance. The CIA is generally associated with investigation of espionage and issues of clandestine operations. ABC, CBS, NBC are relatively new, historically, yet historical letters associated with broadcasting. With the accessibility of cable networking, there are now a myriad of grouped letters that all signify the area of interest in the broadcasting, as in sports, movies, news, etc.

Just as an N following a U indicates association with the United Nations, it is usually recognized that an S following a U pertains to the United States. Our military insignias all include the initials US.

I think the double letter "S" is an enigma that bears mentioning. I simply entered "SS" into the search at acronym finder.com and discovered the double S initials represent 281 different terms. My nine year old granddaughter has now increased that number to 282.

Through our website we have a children's Bible chat hour on Saturday mornings, and she is enjoying using text messaging terms in the chat, such as brb and lol. She now signs on and off with the greeting, "SS," initials for Shabbat Shalom, which is Sabbath peace. In this list of 281, some were quite obscure, but the obvious element for confusion abounds.

To some, "SS" represents Social Security, and to some Selective Service. And through WWII it was associated with the Nazi regime. Often the letters "SS" will lead to internet links addressing Secret Societies which range from college fraternities to recognized organizations of power and wealth, that maintain private membership and alleged, although presumed, rituals. Since the meetings are private and often membership is for life, who will ever know? These examples alone, of only one letter duplicated is only a slight glimpse, but a clear view of potential confusion in meaning.

We are aware that the Social Security System maintains a vast databank in which is recorded and maintained, the work history by annual quarters of all Americans in the work force, and all those that receive a monthly check from the Federal government. This system is huge and rapidly increasing. Unfortunately, we have been told that the outgoing side of the ledger is expected to exceed the incoming, and although the solution is ultimate insolvency, the system is in place, and will remain so, at least regarding collection, probably money, but most assuredly, personal information. These numbers that once were issued at the onset of entering the work force are now issued, although not mandatory, in congruence with a birth certificate. A social security number is not mandatory, but parents cannot claim their children as deductible dependents on a their tax form without a social security number for the child.

The term Selective Service began to be used in the US in 1917 in reference to registration for military availability for all men between the ages of 18-26. It is officially called Selective Service System, and retains all information for each registrant. Although an involuntary military does not exist in this country right now, registration with the Selective Service System is mandatory for all men at the age of 18. Whether it was Germany in the 40's or now in the US, "SS" is associated with protection and/or military, as well as ensuring every adult man is registered in the "system." With a failed ERA, but the rise of feminism, it may be only a matter of time until both genders must register at the age of 18.

Wikipedia explains the term in the following manner: The Selective Service System is the means by which the United States administers military conscription. It entails registering all men between the ages of 18 and 26 with the system for the purpose of having information available about potential soldiers in the event of war. Conscription, however: is defined in WordWeb as: Compulsory military service.

Conscription is compulsory, yet without a draft, there is no compulsory military service. For now, registration is compulsory, but service is not. With the double or triple "S," the definition for the term conscription is now simply open to be defined by usage, as needed.

Most nations around the globe have already established compulsory military service, so as the terminology becomes redefined or undefined by initials, the actual requirements that will be mandated will be a matter of fact reserved behind elusive initials. I believe the term, transparency in government, is already being used in this regard.

Actually, the Social Security System and the Selective Service System already have a combined database for every American male by the age of 26, yet it used to be printed right on the social security card, that it was not intended for ID purposes, and this country has no requirement for mandatory military service, at this time. Clearly, a never ending war will once again require a draft or some sort of mandatory service, first nationally, and ultimately internationally. At this point, in our country, it appears obvious that neither party wants the dubious honor of reinstating what will soon be a necessary draft.

The initials to be watching warily, are "E" and "I."
These are the two letters that tend to appear rather
innocuously in many places at this point, as "E" is the
letter representing ELECTRONIC as in e-banking and e-
mail. "I," of course is the first letter of the word Internet,
which is automatically capitalized in most electronic spell
check programs, including the one I'm using. We have I-
pods and I-phones. But these two letters also appear in
many acronyms and frequently represent the same terms,
although much more ominous in nature. "E," in the
middle of an acronym often indicates the term
EMERGENCY is part of the actual title and "I" continues
to be utilized in initials pertaining to Identity and
Identification.

To a hunter and a politician, the letters NRA mean
Second Amendment Rights and right wing votes; National
Rifle Association. To a chef, these initials may represent
the National Restaurant Association, and to an
occupational therapist, it signifies a professional network,
National Rehabilitation Association. The Naval Reserve
also uses the letters.

The letters DNR . . . On an advanced directive means
Do Not Resuscitate and for those of us that knew about
taking care of the land before the ecologists and
globalists, DNR is the Department of Natural Resources.
There is quite a difference in meaning, therefore; context
is everything. But how is the average citizen going to
keep track of half a million of these overlapping sets of
initials? Sure, when I'm in a hospital DNR means one
thing, but when I'm dealing with the government, it's
another matter all together but, when the government and
health care are
combined . . . Will there be new initials or will we
someday have the order on our health care chart, Do Not
Resuscitate, because we have exceeded our entitled

allotment from the Department of Natural Resources?

It's all about words. Since we have chosen to eliminate G-d's Word from the "public square," which is the actual living and interaction in this country, we have replaced His Word with a plethora of words, letters and laws that are merely confusion.

G-d is not the author of confusion.

A general rule of thumb, although it is not absolute, is when an acronym or "monogram" ends in "A," the "A," by and large, stands for one of several things; Association, Agency, Administration, or America. Act is now also a term represented by "A," usually at the end of an acronym and usually signifying some sort of legislation, already in place.

"D" frequently designates, Department, but also Division.

"N" is usually a reference for the term, National.

As I mentioned earlier. When "E" is at the beginning, it is primarily a reference to the technological term "electronic." When it occurs later in the acronym it often represents the word, emergency, in some sort of emergency response solution, agency, or bureaucracy.

The letter "G" is a bit tricky, as it can refer to Global, Government, or General. Ultimately, it would appear that those terms will, in many ways, become interchangeable.

The (.gov) sites are all US government related. Also, although not exclusively, the domain sites that are (.us) are also often associated with the US government, but all sites with the (.us) either originate or are contained, at this time, within the United States. Usually the combined letters of U and S represent the United States and when the letter A follows, it is generally presumed to represent the word America. In the case of the USA PATRIOT Act, however: this general rule of thumb does not apply. In this particular acronym, US does not stand for United States. The term represented in this letter grouping is included in the list of acronyms at the end of this chapter.

The list of possible confusing initials and acronyms is virtually endless, but I will address one more that just won't leave my awareness. It's almost as if we're bombarded with a term that just gets tacked on the end of many public service announcements and that is the term, *ad hoc* or ADHOC. When it's radio, I can't tell which word is referred to and since it is usually mentioned pertaining to a committee or sponsorship, I still cannot discern the connection. The term *ad hoc* is Latin, meaning, for this purpose. The initials ADHOC refer to a human rights organization. It is used frequently in reference to the formation of committees on a local government level, yet the UN has a number of *ad hoc* committees to address and research an abundance of global concerns. It appears that every level of government has their *ad hoc* committees and bureaucracies "for the purpose" and/or for human rights. ADHOC or *ad hoc* is a very nebulous term. AD HOC is a redundant paradox, thus by definition, an absolute absurdity. Humans were not created to answer to the governments, but rather, governments were established to protect the rights of humans. Human rights are supposed to be the purpose of the local government all the way to the UN.

The political terminology for peace negotiations is "agreeing on wording." It's so much easier to agree upon wording, when acronyms come into play. When initials and letters that begin as abbreviated references actually become the terms, the original words fade, or the vagueness of the initials camouflage the terminology, as it was contained in the original definition. The primary information that was first introduced, will eventually become irrelevant or simply confused. As the power and presence of the bureaucracy, organization, or technology become the actual focus, and the people simply accept the "word" of the powers that it is in their best interest. Acronyms provide an elusive transparency for those in authority.

For a number of years, I expected the "mark" to be a tatoo or indelible image of some sort on the skin, which it still may be, but I have certainly come to understand, this "mark" could be and in all probability will be an all inclusive, technological connection between each individual and the monocracy.

Interestingly, when I looked up "666" in the Greek portion of the Strong's Exhaustive Concordance, there was a reference to letters with that numerical value. The alphabet of Hebrew and Ancient Greek were both numerical as well as linguistic. Each letter, of course represented a particular sound, but also signified a numerical value. The English letters U, V, and W are all translated from this Hebrew letter, "ו" (vav) It has the value of 6 in Hebrew and incidentally, when I changed from this font to the Hebrew, the "W" key produced "ו." Considering the dependence on technology and the love of money, the potential for 666 to correlate with www. is certainly a possibility.

The explanation in the Greek portion of James Strong's work, indicates these letters that were first written are rather difficult to pinpoint, as they may have been letters that have since become obsolete. Perhaps they were letters that simply represented more than was readily recognized.

The "mark" could be an electronic chip, since it could be encoded with both letters and numbers, and placed within the human body, and accessed technologically.

The "mark" could be contained in the title of the epicenter of provision, as contained in the term 'market.' The "mark" could also be an acronym. And the word mark can also be spelled with a "C."

The mark or marc can certainly be "all of the above." A Google Search on the letters MARC was informative, but I'm sure the data will update and expand regularly, until the time of the end. The Multiple Agency Resource Center, a.k.a. MARC; also shares the acronym for the Mutual Aid Regional Coordination.

At this point and so far, the "C" of the MARC appears to represent Center or Coordination, both of which elude to two more "C" words. A community in need or working together under a crisis type of reference. The place that provides or connects to whatever is needed. The MARC of the beast may simply be the accepted and permanent sign of entitlement, be it electronic medical chips, traceable chips for safety, or identifying technology for SMART transactions or travel.

We must keep in mind, the prophecies contained in the book of Daniel. There are many individuals who have been led to believe there is going to suddenly be some sort of bizarre monster with 7 heads and 10 horns, giving a choice of bowing down or death. The Scriptural reference to governments in Daniel's dream and the interpretation given was the term and description of beasts. Heads can be officials and horns can be powers or even powerful departments.

The MARC will be the indelible insignia required for transactions and recognized as tractable. Just a side note. There is only one letter difference between traceable and tractable, but the implications are diametrical.

Ultimately the power of the New World Order will insist upon tracking, observing, and monitoring everyone. There will be a small minority, however; that are less than cooperative, which at some point will simply face death as defiant dissidents. Of course, there will always be those, for the promise of comfort or convenience, security and safety, who truly believe they should be compliant. Many people, world wide, devoutly believe in their governments. The official transition from global cooperation to One World Order will be so subtle, most will surrender to the marc or mark of the beast, long before it is mandated. This mark will enable any and every one to be accommodated to receive any and every thing they "need," and in a time of need and fear, this will be established. SMART is the best example for the crux of this text. S.M.A.R.T. stands for Self Monitoring Analysis and Reporting Technology, but simply means all those that willingly comply and rely, are merely tractable.

In this chapter I would like to include a number of initials and letter groupings that we have become familiar with, as well as those that are being introduced into the global lexicon. These terms are not limited to English or exclusive to America, although once again, this is where I am and this is where I hear them, but many do in fact, have global recognition.

Here are a few words made of the "old" acronyms that have become so familiar, they are now actually recognized as English words in Webster's Dictionary. Not only have each of these become words of common use signifying their original description, but these words, now, also have definition.

Laser: Light Amplification by Stimulated Emission of Radiation

Laser is now a reference to a beam of light specifically related to a number of medical procedures.

Radar: RAdio Detection And Ranging.

Radar is now defined as a measuring instrument.

Sonar: SOund NAvigation and Ranging

Sonar is a technique that uses sound propagation under water to communicate or detect.

Just a few short years ago, with the technological advancement and discovery in the area of light and sound, these acronyms were introduced as labels describing the process, and now they are simply recognized as the function.

I've listed just a few of the acronyms, terms, and initials that I believe we will be seeing and hearing much more about in the days to come.

GSA   General Services Administration
UNESCO   United Nations Educational, Scientific, and
                              Cultural Organization
UNICEF   United Nations Children's Fund.
the "I" and "E" do not represent words, at this time.
GPS   Global Positioning Satellite
CALEA   Communication Assistance for Law
Enforcement Act
e-mail   electronic mail through the internet
ADHOC   human rights organization
ad hoc   for this purpose (Latin)
CHIP Children's Health Insurance Program
CHIP Children's Hospital Informatics Program *
NSA   National Security Agency
CIVPOL   Civilian Police
NAIS   National Animal Identification System
UN   United Nations
EPA   Environmental Protection Agency
FEMA Federal Emergency Management Agency
SS   Social Security
SS   Selective Service
SEMA State Emergency Management Agency
RFID Radio Frequency Identification (ID)
HUD Housing and Urban Development
NASA National Aeronautics and Space Administration
USMC United States Marine Corps
CBS has so many possibilities, wikipedia recommended
another page for disambiguation

USA United States of America
CIA Central Intelligence Agency
USN United States Navy
USN Universal Space Network
FBI Federal Bureau of Investigation
USAF United States Air Force
IRS Internal Revenue Service
USDA United States Department of Agriculture
FDA Food and Drug Administration
FD (usually follows city initials) Fire Department
PD (usually follows city initials) Police Department
CNN Cable News Network
UNIPOL Universal Police
INTERPOL International Criminal Police Organization -
ICPO. Although I can't really say what this organization
does, as the title alone, I find confusing. My research
clearly specified that this organization is world wide with
over 180 members, the US included, and is not to be
confused with the International Police. International
Police is a different association, usually serving in areas
torn by war, often referred to as Peacekeepers.
FISA Foreign Intelligence Surveillance Act
I believe FISA will soon change. Either the same letters
will represent more words, or this acronym will become
obsolete to it's original definition under expansion, or it
will become a word unto itself. As this statute continues
to become a greater part of domestic legislation and
homeland procedures, it will just become a term in which
the original words are irrelevant. With a global
government, the word, foreign, will become redefined.
Internet: A worldwide, publicly accessible series of
interconnected computer networks.
I-pod: I is a computer reference, portable, player that
digitally records, rips, and plays, music.
I-phone: Internet enabled, multimedia, mobile phone.

Although the A still stands for America, this is the exception to the rule of thumb regarding the initials US: USA PATRIOT Act: <u>Uniting and Strengthening</u> America by Providing Appropriate Tools Required to Intercept and Obstruct Terrorism Act of 2001. This is the one branch of technocracy that has already invaded our privacy and will continue to maintain our society and monitor our moves. It will, of course, be for our safety and concern for the children.

COBRA is one of my biggest pet peeves in acronyms. Consolidated Omnibus Budget Reconciliation Act. The health benefit provisions, passed by Congress, in 1986. The law amends the Employee Retirement Income Security Act, the Internal Revenue Code, and the Public Health Service Act to provide continuation of group health coverage that otherwise might be terminated.

Government guaranteed health care in association with a term for a serpent.

* The "I" in the second acronym of CHIP in the list, is the first letter of the word, informatics. Informatics is defined as the sciences concerned with gathering, manipulating, storing, retrieving, and classifying recorded information. I found, manipulating, to be an odd term in the midst of the other words used in the definition.

When a civilization becomes so fast paced and high tech, that entire sentences must be condensed into single code words, the original term and meaning, bears the potential or even intent to be lost, misconstrued, or expounded upon in a variety of directions, or possibly manipulated.

How can we be so certain of meaning of content with just a letter? Context! Of course, we have the context to let us know, but does context truly resolve debatable interpretation? Context of Scripture has resulted in just how many interpretations and denominations? G-d's Word is absolute truth. That certainly cannot be said regarding this "technolese." We know many acronyms are nothing more than technological codes to be integrated into the present culture as the subtle transformation continues to proceed.

When every letter stands for a complete word or words that are assumed by the circumstances and context, acronyms pave the way for assignment rather than assessment. It creates it's own set of absolutes by automatic association rather than analysis and understanding. Acronyms severely diminish our lexicon.

And the whole earth was of one language, and of one speech.
Genesis 11: 1

In the abundance of words transgression ceaseth not . . .
Proverbs 10: 19

A is for apple, appaloosa, aggravated, acronym, agenda, and accountability . . . Just to name a few.

A is also for **apocalypse**.

For the great day of His wrath is come; and who shall be able to stand?
Revelation 6: 17

Chapter 25

The Doorway to Despotism

Despotism is a form of government in which the ruler is an absolute dictator (not restricted by a constitution, laws, or opposition, etc), also known as a monocracy. I realize even the possibility of this sounds pretty far fetched, yet Scripture perfectly and accurately prophesies this very government. This government will be put in place by the will of the People. When the government of the beast is in full control there will be no opposition to that government without penalty. One of the strongest transitional points that will be virtually indiscernible is the transition of Constitutional Law to a vague, general Rule of Law, as many countries are revising their constitutions, or treating them as historic documents. Although Constitutions are not set in stone, they are not living documents, either. They should not be easily revised or amended. Unfortunately, without some amendments, they become antiquated and potentially obsolete to the culture. A Constitution is in the hands of man. Only G-d's Word is both set in stone and living.

America is not the only country that espouses this well used term, "Rule of Law," making it all the more frightening. There are many nations in which their tribulations and triumphs are global headlines. We've read only recently about the election in Pakistan between the two parties. We read about the dissatisfaction of some members of that society, to the point of assassination. Israel has more than one party, and is once again having an extra primary election. France and Russia just recently changed leaders, as did Germany not long ago. The one thing that we fail to see in other nations is the every day workings, because the everyday workings are not considered international headline making news. The American political scene, however; does make international headlines and will contribute in one way or another as the New World Order takes shape.

Although this is becoming a global issue, it is clear to see the subtlety when viewed one country at a time, and my best vantage point is, of course, my own country. Whether it's Republican Reciprocity or Democratic Dichotomy, we are going to see more and more rules that defy reason, by virtue of unenforced legislation that already exists and amendments for statutes that are nonexistent for our "safe protection" as a society. This is not just a republican/democrat situation, as we can see it to some degree in other lands. As the world heads for one world government, is America going along or leading the way? Either way, the destination is the same.

I've noticed several public service announcements on the radio mention their sponsors at the end of the information given, and usually the Ad Council is mentioned. I wasn't exactly sure just what the Ad Council was, so I did a quick search of it's home page. This organization has been around since WWII. I've included the mission statement and tag line found on the home page of the Ad Council.

Mission

Our mission is to identify a select number of significant public issues and stimulate action on those issues through communications programs that make a measurable difference in our society.

The Ad Council is a private, non-profit organization that marshals volunteer talent from the advertising and communications industries, the facilities of the media, and the resources of the business and non-profit communities to deliver critical messages to the American public. The Ad Council produces, distributes and promotes thousands of public service campaigns on behalf of non-profit organizations and government agencies in issue areas such as improving the quality of life for children, preventative health, education, community well being, environmental preservation and strengthening families.

A review of the Ad Council's campaign dockets through the years demonstrates the organization's commitment to address the most pressing social issues of the day. To that end, the Ad Council campaign docket is adjusted to mirror changes in our society. However, although the docket changes, the organization's commitment to the nation and to its people remains clear and constant.

Ad Council icons and slogans are woven into the very fabric of American culture -- Smokey Bear's "Only You Can Prevent Forest Fires," The Crash Test Dummies: "You Could Learn A lot from a Dummy,"

215

McGruff the Crime Dog's: "Take A Bite Out of Crime," and of course, "A Mind is a Terrible Thing To Waste," and "Friends Don't Let Friends Drive Drunk" - just to name a few.

It's All about The Results!

Although most Americans can assuredly recite Ad Council slogans, Ad Council PSAs are not just memorized. They mobilize. The results of our campaigns testify to the power of the Ad Council's messages to make lasting and positive social change. Results such as these inspire the Ad Council to continue the work of its founders and rouse the passion of its successors to ensure that future generations of Americans will flourish from the positive changes the Ad Council has initiated.

Although the ad council claims to be a private organization that promotes public service campaigns, when I visited the webpage, it is clear to see that many of these campaigns have resulted in legislation. Since 1942, has the ad council campaigned to raise awareness of issues in our society, or rallied and programmed the people to ask for more laws?

I've wondered for years as our politicians vie and contend through campaigns, when the party in power changes, why the "mistakes" of the last administration do not get corrected. When a Republican is in office and the Democrats are disgruntled, when the Democrat is elected, why doesn't that leader repeal what the Republican did? And when Republicans disapprove of decisions by a Democratic administration, why not repair or amend those previous decisions, when they take office? Why doesn't anything change when party leadership does? The answer is unfortunately simple. Humanity cannot fix the world's problems, politically or militarily, and we certainly can't

216

buy our way out of the mess. We can only change leaders, declare wars, and throw money at the ills of humanity, but we cannot restore this world to the paradise that G-d created it to be.

John Adams is quoted as saying in his writings, <u>Thoughts on Government</u>, "the very definition of a republic is an empire of laws and not of man." How long will the subtle segue take, as we go from a republic by the rule of law to an Empire? Some of us are already using the term, in unhappy recognition. In all the progress of humanity, we have now arrived at this catchy phrase heard from America to Saudi Arabia, "The Rule of Law." I am amazed and somewhat dismayed at the number of Arab nations that are republics of one kind or another. We must remember that there truly is no Western democracy as America is also a republic.

Any and all types of government are ultimately potential monocracies, but the technocratic governments will lead the global race, clearly seen through much of the last Century. Even the arms race is an "arm" of technological world competition. Every nation on the planet is led or supported by technocrats from arms to communication to the genetically modified food, flown in to third world countries. Technology is the absolute power of humanity for the 21st Century and a technocracy will make the move to a monocracy or despotism happen subtly, rather than suddenly.

The foundational pieces are already in place, have been for years, and certainly gaining our dependence.

When we use the phone in any commercial purpose we surrender to technology just to actually speak with a live person. We compliantly obey the prompts, and accept the knowledge that we have no other recourse for resolution. We know now, whether it's a department store, a government office, or even the phone company itself, all hope of obtaining a live voice on the other end of the line, rests upon our accurate obedience to the technological commands. I've often wondered if I spend as much time in prayer to G-d who actually answers, as I do on hold and going through the prompts.

After the US invasion of Afghanistan, the goat herders were brought into the 21st century with cell phones. Following the US invasion of Iraq, the first things the "freed" Iraqis wanted, were satellites and televisions.

There is no doubt, world leaders, all want to remain powerful. The laws that are changing are taking the freedom out of the hands of people, world wide, all in the name of safety, because there is great power in the incitement of fear. As we are coming to realize, there is even greater power in providing surveillance and protection through technology.

Now that we have all this protection and surveillance against terror . . . and the punishment no longer fits the crime, G-d help us all when the crimes start fitting the punishment.

I read about a 10 year old girl that was arrested for having a knife at school. Her mother had packed it in her lunch to cut her steak. Maybe her mom hadn't thought that through very carefully, but the little girl was not threatening anyone and was just sitting at the lunch table, when a teacher made the decision to make it a legal matter. Where is the reason? What is this teacher going to do when a real problem occurs? Is this the mentality of those that are entrusted to teach our children?

A 6 year old boy has been labeled, a sex offender, because he kissed a 6 year old girl, at school. The child's father said he didn't have any idea how to even explain this to the child. Granted, children are exposed to too much entirely too early, but first graders have experienced puppy love and fear of "cooties" for decades. Does anyone really feel safer, knowing this child has been labeled in such a way?

It's nearly impossible to even read the headlines today without reading about some little boy being reprimanded or suspended for sketching a gun or knife.

Since we, as a society, have decided to become extreme, why don't we just stop making all the "kill 'em up' video games and strange weapons for cartoon villains and super heroes? I realize, it has been determined that it takes an entire village to raise a child, but we simply must recognize the number of village idiots and restrict their influence and/or authority.

Now that these children have already been treated as criminals, where will the rationale be, when faced with real decisions of right and wrong?

Since America has reveled in it's own rule of law in the name of freedom, while religiously disregarding G-d's Law because of grace and freedom, the following laws of reciprocity will be demonstrated throughout this culture and society.

G-d's Word says in *I John 4: 18 "...Perfect love casts out fear..."* and earlier in the 4th Chapter of I John, can be found the words, *"G-d is love."* It would therefore follow, reciprocally, that fear exists in the absence of G-d. Bible believers should know nothing good will result in fear-mongering, because fear of evil does not invite the presence of G-d. History has demonstrated, societies that believe in their own might and military power, live in perpetual fear and constant vigilance of being challenged or attacked. History has also taught us, these nations have become history. History should have also taught us, if might and military power did preserve governments, a nation as new as America would not have become the super power that it did. All the old might and military would have prevented it.

History has also demonstrated that fear is a powerful tool used to control a society and coerce entire nations into all sorts of acts of patriotism. G-d's Word has given a very clear and concise description of the consequences in establishing this type of society.

The Revelation states in 13: 10 *"those that lead into captivity will go into captivity and those that kill by the sword must die by the sword."* His Word also tells us, it's repeated, in many passages to *"Fear not."* Just what is faithful, healthy fear?

Following the warning in regard to patriotic panic, I'd like to mention the Scriptural Instruction found in Isaiah. I always found it offensive when preachers and teachers presented spiritual matters to be emotional, yet absent of the use of intelligence, as if the brain and soul were in opposition. We should be intelligent enough to know, that is not the case.

"Come let us reason together . . ." Isaiah 1: 18.

There is promise after promise in Scripture that G-d takes care of His people, and He will bring them through in victory. Our definition of victory and care may not be the same thing He has planned, however. We need to seek Him to see. G-d actually has given us an opportunity to sit and talk with Him, to hear Him and be heard by Him. To leave G-d out is to abandon reason. To attempt to portray intellect and spirit in opposition is to reject the truth that we are created in the image of G-d. I have no doubt that G-d, who is Spirit, is both logical and intellectual.

We have a wonderful promise found in the account of the Gospel according to John. *He who the Son sets free is free indeed. John 8: 36*

As for earthly powers declaring freedom . . .

If the rule of law defines our Constitutional freedoms, then G-d's Law defines our spiritual freedom.

Unfortunately, there is already a Directive on "the books" that make provision for a temporary suspension of our constitutional government. This special Directive allows for "coordinated continuity in the case of crisis," with a distinct power shift outside of the ascribed method penned in our Constitution. If the United States has this alternative in place, clearly the governments throughout the world that are not operating within the parameters of a Constitution are already closer to their position in a One World Government. There are many governments that will not need to defer to a Directive 51 to take their place in the New World Order.

The Rule of Law does not necessarily require a Constitution, a Congress, or a Parliament. As John Adams made clear in the quote I included, the Rule of Law is not an empire of man, but he did define it to be an empire, none the less. The rule of law only requires an individual that has enough or will assume enough authority to enforce it. "Of the people, by the people, and for the people" is only contained in Lincoln's Gettysburg Address, not in the UN by-laws, not in the Constitution of the United States, and not in Directive 51, dated May of 2007.

In the same hour came forth fingers of a man's hand, and wrote over against the candlestick upon the plaster of the wall of the king's palace: and the king saw the part of the hand that wrote. --- And this is the writing that was written, MENE, MENE, TEKEL, UPHARSIN. This is the interpretation of the thing: MENE; God hath numbered thy kingdom, and finished it. TEKEL; Thou art weighed in the balances, and art found wanting.
Daniel 5: 5, 25-27

Ye shall not do after all the things that we do here this day, every man whatsoever is right in his own eyes.
Deuteronomy 12: 8

You shall know the truth and the truth shall make you free. *John 8: 32*

Without the truth are we kept in captivity? If the truth makes one free? Then deception confines.

    With regard to the word "confine," we haven't yet begun to experience the vague, yet vast meaning of Rule of Law.

So speak ye, and so do, as they that shall be judged by the law of liberty. *James 2: 12*

And it was given unto him to make war with the saints, and to overcome them: and power was given him over all kindreds, and tongues, and nations. And all that dwell upon the earth shall worship him, whose names are not written in the book of life of the Lamb slain from the foundation of the world.
Revelation 13: 7, 8

Chapter 26

As In the Days of Noah. . .

Heavy rain is frequently associated with the name of Noah. Many big weather events, today, are described as "in Biblical proportion," yet while we are looking out the window and talking about the weather, so much more is taking place.

When Y'hshuwah uttered the words, "as in the days of Noah," nearly 2000 years ago, I doubt that those listening had any idea what an encompassing statement they were hearing. I've read that passage for years, now, and as world events continue to unfold I see the meaning of the statement, being revealed in greater magnitude, almost daily. First, though, my duty as a servant of YHWH is to proclaim the Good News. In Genesis 6: 8, we find the first place the word grace appears in Scripture. *Noah found grace in the eyes of YHWH.* And, so as in the days of Noah, the grace of G-d can still be found.

There is, however; a sad verse right before we read where Noah is given the instructions.

Genesis 6: 6 says that G-d's creation of man caused Him sorrow. G-d was sorry He made humans!

I'd have to say, whether believers or unbelievers, there is near universal recognition of the name of Noah. I've never met a person that didn't know what the ark was and it doesn't take much rain to hear someone make a comment in regard to building a boat. Even though a large portion of society has discounted the account of the great flood, altogether, it is clear to see that inclement weather gets the attention of man, around the world.

I can't count the number of times I've heard the term "in Biblical proportion" used, as of late. There are rains, local floods, weather alarm radios called NOAA radios (pronounced Noah), comments regarding building an ark, animal shelters either referring to Noah in the title, or the full name of the organization bearing the acronym of NOAH. I also discovered the Neighborhood of Affordable Housing and New York Online Access to Health uses the acronym of NOAH.

The passage of Scripture pertaining to Noah is not terribly lengthy. His lifespan, ark, flood and all, is contained in about five chapters of Genesis, but there are a number of statements in that portion that Y'hshuwah made reference to "as in the days of Noah." These are registering rather significantly in my awareness as they are revealed in these last days. There is a passage in Genesis 6 that says the life expectancy of man is to be 120 years. Recently we heard some sort of radio sales program, with the promoter mentioning a marketing "epiphany" as he offered a vast array of expensive health elixirs, while telling his listening audience that we are supposed to live 120 years. Not to mention, the term epiphany, used to be a reference to a vision of Messiah.

When Y'hshuwah made reference to the days of Noah, who knew there would be a "religious/society" develop, complete with governmental laws and punishments, supposedly named for Noah? There is a growing community of individuals in many places in the world, striving to be righteous Gentiles, as defined by the Chabad Lubavitch movement, known as Noahides or "sons of Noah."

The deceased Chabad Lubavitch leader has been quite influential, on occasion in the White House, and to this day his memory and teachings are still influential throughout Judaism, as well as appointed officials of the U.S. government.

Now, as to the Days of Noah. We know the world was corrupt and we know that there was a reference to sons of G-d and daughters of man, so there was a recognition of religion at that time, but a serious combining of tradition and cultures with spirituality and religion, apparently without truth; and clearly without G-d's favor.

The three major world religions will ultimately embrace the monocracy based upon these seven laws for the very simple reasons that appeal to their already established laws and belief system. As I have already mentioned, all three religions share the first 16 chapters of Genesis foundationally in their religions, which also include the complete account of Noah. Some are already aware that it has the potential to empower a government of seven laws, of course with sub statutes. Could this be the government described in Revelation 13, as the beast having seven heads? This belief system or lifestyle has been "creatively" established using seven verses, upon which I will elaborate just a bit. I first learned of this religious / government, when President George Bush introduced this on "Education Day" in 1991. In my research I came across the day in which Ronald Reagan referenced this same set of laws, nearly a decade earlier, in 1982, commemorating it "Day of Reflection."

Some Christian watch groups quote the former President as saying the Noahide laws have been the "bedrock of society from the dawn of civilization." I have included, later in this chapter, the quote from President Bush's speech, as well as the governmental site in which I found the document. It was also President George Bush speaking, when I first heard the term New World Order, as he shared the vision for our nation in the global economy.

These Noahide Laws, as they are called, will ultimately be a win/win/win for the religious influence that is so desired in politics today by the extremists of each religion. Christians will reach out for the presumed "Bible based" morality, legal statutes, and consequences.
Muslims will espouse the power of unification and the death sentence to the infidels.
The Jews will savor the authority and recognition of judiciary dominance amidst the nations.

Scripture describes the beastly government as having seven heads. The Noahide laws number seven. Six laws regard the conduct of society, and one law designates officials to enforce them. All religions and many non-religious will agree that these laws are basic to society, but they are not straight out of Scripture verbatim. They are, rather, a loose translation from Talmud, claiming Scriptural authority. As societies become motivated by hostility and moved by argument, these "seven laws" will be accepted on the mere ground, "There is no argument against them."

Below, you'll find a list of the regulations and the commands prohibiting the specifics found in Scripture. The punishment and description of justice, however; are not found in Scripture nor are many of the interpreted details. The punishment for breaking most any of these seven laws is primarily capital punishment by decapitation. Most offenses are punishable by death. There is enough capital punishment contained in this "bedrock of society" to meet the approval of both Iran and Texas.

The seven laws for righteous Gentiles, acknowledged by the Talmud are

Prohibition of Idolatry: There is only one G-d. You shall not make for yourself an idol.

Prohibition of Murder: You shall not murder.

Prohibition of Theft: You shall not steal.

Prohibition of Sexual Promiscuity: You shall not commit adultery.

Prohibition of Blasphemy: Revere G-d and do not blaspheme.

Prohibition of Cruelty to Animals: Do not eat flesh taken from an animal while it is still alive.

Requirement to have just Laws You shall set up an effective judiciary to fairly judge observance of the preceding six laws.

There are ultimately 66 sub laws to be observed by the "righteous Gentiles," and when one breaks down the Seven Laws of Noah, it is explained that there are actually six laws of prohibition and one law of requirement, to enforce the six. Chabad presents the Noahide legal system to be of the G-d of Israel and containing the perfect number of completion, which is seven.

In the actual breakdown of this Talmudic based legal system, there is one regulating force to enforce 6 laws, containing 66 sub-laws. Revelation 13 mentions the number 6, three times, and the correlation, thereof.

Here is the list of Scriptural references and order of laws listed at www.bnainoah.net, used to justify this

particular legal system known as the Seven Laws of Noah.
1. Do not utter G-d's name in vain; curse G-d, or pursue the occult. Genesis 3: 1
2. Do not worship false gods/idols. Genesis 3: 5
3. Do not steal or kidnap. Genesis 3: 6
4. Do not murder. Genesis 4: 8
5. Do not be sexually immoral (engage in incest, sodomy, bestiality, homosexuality, castration, and adultery)
Genesis 6: 1-4
6. Set up righteous and honest courts and apply fair justice in judging offenders and uphold the principles of the last five. Genesis 6: 5-7
7. Do not eat a part of a live animal. Genesis 9 : 3-4

Clearly, these are valuable statutes to govern a society. The problem lies in the presumed connotation. Although, we are familiar with the fact, the Ten Commandments cover much of this, I found many of the interpretations from these particular Scriptural references to be a bit of an interpretive, retrospective stretch.

1. *Genesis 3: 1 Now the serpent was more subtle than any beast of the field which the LORD G-d had made. And he said unto the woman, Yea, hath G-d said, Ye shall not eat of every tree of the garden?*

2. *Genesis 3: 5 For G-d doth know that in the day ye eat thereof, then your eyes shall be opened, and ye shall be as gods, knowing good and evil.*
Did you notice that both of these Scriptural references quoted are the words of the serpent? The first two verses used to justify these laws are words uttered, not by G-d, but by the serpent.

3. *Genesis 3: 6 And when the woman saw that the tree*

was good for food, and that it was pleasant to the eyes, and a tree to be desired to make one wise, she took of the fruit thereof, and did eat, and gave also unto her husband with her; and he did eat.

Stealing . . . I can see that. They were told to leave that fruit alone, so it was not left to their discretionary choice, it was not their right to pick and partake, but kidnapping?

Granted, kidnapping is wrong and Torah more than implies that fact, but it's well beyond a stretch to find it in this verse.

4. *Genesis 4: 8 And Cain talked with Abel his brother: and it came to pass, when they were in the field, that Cain rose up against Abel his brother, and slew him.*

Murder has been wrong, obviously from the beginning, and yet throughout history, humanity has justified the taking of human life in many ways, and will continue to do so.

5. *Genesis 6: 1-4 And it came to pass, when men began to multiply on the face of the earth, and daughters were born unto them, That the sons of G-d saw the daughters of men that they were fair; and they took them wives of all which they chose. And the LORD said, My spirit shall not always strive with man, for that he also is flesh: yet his days shall be an hundred and twenty years. There were giants in the earth in those days; and also after that, when the sons of G-d came in unto the daughters of men, and they bare children to them, the same became mighty men which were of old, men of renown.*

There is a lengthy list of sexual sins, which once appear listed in Torah and forbidden, but this verse does not stand alone to prohibit the list mentioned in the Noahide List. As a matter of fact, this verse describes exactly what is legal now in our country. People choose their partner in marriage and that decision is frequently based upon looks, while faith and beliefs are often secondary, or even considered to be completely unimportant and irrelevant.

6. *Genesis 6: 5-7 And G-d saw that the wickedness of man was great in the earth, and that every imagination of the thoughts of his heart was only evil continually. And it repented the LORD that he had made man on the earth, and it grieved him at his heart. And the LORD said, I will destroy man whom I have created from the face of the earth; both man, and beast, and the creeping thing, and the fowls of the air; for it repenteth me that I have made them.*

Most people that are familiar with Scripture know this is the passage that first introduces G-d's plan for a world wide flood. His plan for judges didn't enter the picture until the time of Moses. But if you'll notice, "I will destroy man whom I have created from the face of the earth;" is the reference used by Chabad and Noahide to justify murder, calling it capital punishment, as the judges of this belief system determine what is just, and exact their interpretation of justice.

That will be the problem with the vastly detailed interpretation, yet unwritten regulation in this rule of law. Many will find themselves at the mercy of an absolutely authoritarian, unmerciful government.

Genesis 9: 3-4 Every moving thing that liveth shall be meat for you; even as the green herb have I given you all things. But flesh with the life thereof, which is the blood thereof, shall ye not eat.

I certainly would never attempt to make an argument in favor of eating a part of any animal that is still alive, but there are a number of rules and regulations, unwritten in this belief system, that specify how an animal is to be slaughtered and if it is done incorrectly, this is determined to be animal cruelty, which is also included in this statute, according to Talmud.

It is the humble opinion of the author that without the rest of the Five Books of Torah, these individual verses are not as direct and concise in understanding as the religious/government will insist. Outside of Messiah, there is none righteous. As the Pharisees have already historically demonstrated, man's interpretation and elaboration often distort the context of the truth of G-d. Usually the distortion begins as a self-righteous effort to exercise authority and judgment beyond what G-d has ordained to be carried out by the hand of humanity.

Is the beast with seven heads, mentioned in the Revelation, this Noahide government with seven laws and judges? We need only to look around to see these laws already being subtly put in place with the accolades of the masses, and rightfully so, for now. These laws are presented to be quite simple and clear in nature, but the end results and obscure interpretations will be far from what is presented now. The specific examples cited, presently by Chabad and Noahide are only one of many statutes under each of the Seven General Laws.

Many Christian groups are savvy to this rising tide, but there is deceptive discussion in which the Chabad outreach effort is addressing the possibility to initially embrace Trinitarianism. Some Noahide groups indicate their belief that Christians are technically not committing idolatry when they worship Jesus, if they believe in the Trinity. A very revered Sage of Judaism, Maimonides 1135-1204 C.E., claimed that Islam does not practice idolatry, and I've already mentioned that Chabad is not considered a separate branch of Judaism but recognized and acknowledged by many in Orthodox, Conservative, and Reform.

The Chabad and Noahide movement have extended a great deal of outreach energy in an effort to embrace and include factions of all religions. They do, however; take full exception and find total disdain with one specific group of people. That group is comprised of those individuals who acknowledge One G-d, observe Torah Instruction, Keep the Commandments, commemorate Sabbath, celebrate Holy Days, and follow Messiah.
And the dragon was wroth with the woman, and went to make war with the remnant of her seed, which keep the commandments of G-d, and have the testimony of Y'hshuwah Messiah. Revelation 12: 17

The President of the United States has already declared and documented a legal foundation for this government to stand.
[105 STAT. 44 Public Law 102□14 □□ March 20, 1991 Joint Resolution To designate March 26, 1991, as "Education Day, U.S.A."
Whereas Congress recognizes the historical tradition of ethical values and principles which are the basis of civilized society and upon which our great Nation was founded;
Whereas these ethical values and principles have been the bedrock of society from the dawn of civilization, when they were known as the Seven Noahide Laws;
Whereas without these ethical values and principles the edifice of civilization stands in serious peril of returning chaos;
Whereas society is profoundly concerned with the recent weakening of these principles that has resulted in crises that beleaguer and threaten the fabric of civilized society; . . .]

Check Library of Congress.gov   Thomas section

Could this be a sign and work done by a spirit of anti-christ? Not only did this become documented by the agreement of a Republican President and Democratic Congress without gridlock, but no atheists, agnostics, or humanists protested the reference to Noah, either.
Public Law 102-14

It will be called ordained. After all, there are seven verses of Scripture mentioned, and Romans 13 tells us all governments are ordained of G-d.

Even though, this may appear to only have taken place in the United States, we need to remember these seven laws are already accepted by the three main religions of the world.

Just another interesting note in regard to the date of this Public Law 102-14. The Congress that approved President Bush's declaration and Joint Resolution was also the first Congress to have a Muslim Imam open with prayer, that same year.

The laws contained in America's Public Law 102-14 referred to as the Seven Noahide Laws and the Talmudic Law of Judaism as explained by the Chabad Lubavitch movement to define and govern the "righteous Gentiles," are also in agreement with the Sha'ria law of Islam.

Y'hshuwah's comments regarding the days of Noah, cover as much ground as the flood did. Marriage is based on much the same perspective as in the days of Noah, physical attractiveness and personal choice, rather than G-d's direction. According to Genesis 10: 25, the land mass of the earth was still connected at the time of the flood. We now have global travel and world wide communication. Technology has reconnected the continents. More similarities, contained in this simple statement by Messiah, will continue to be revealed, I'm sure.

The ark was no small dinghy. The time it took to build it and the massive space it covered on dry land, surely gave cause to raise questions, at least for onlookers and bystanders to take notice. There is one factor that we simply can't overlook in the parallel drawn by Messiah to "as in the days of Noah;" the majority freely elected to "miss the boat!"

And as it was in the days of Noah, so shall it be also in the days of the Son of man. They did eat, they drank, they married wives, they were given in marriage, until the day that Noah entered into the ark, and the flood came, and destroyed them all.
Luke 17: 26, 27

Then said these men, We shall not find any occasion against this Daniel, except we find it against him concerning the law of his G-d.
Daniel 6: 5

And I looked, and, lo, a Lamb stood on the mount Zion, and with him an hundred forty and four thousand, having his Father's name written in their foreheads.
Revelation 14: 1

the Last Chapter

. . . It is finished . . .
John 19: 30

There are some days, I would just like to be able to write a pleasant popular book, what the crowd wants to hear, but I know that isn't to be my priority. I frequently tell my daughter and husband, "I'm writing another 'best' worst seller." Noah didn't have a popular message or simple task. It is said that Jeremiah never saw a convert. Many are saying what the crowds want to hear, specifically the religious crowd. If Y'hshuwah had just said what the Pharisees wanted to hear, how would history have been changed?

Instead, he was busy about his Father's business. He brought sight to the blind, deliverance to those in bondage, freedom to the captive; He gave living water to those that thirsted and spoke life to the perishing.

His words were lunacy to the secular and heresy to the religious.

He said, ***I came to do the will of my Father. John 5: 30***

    With all the evil in the world, there is still a message of good news. Bad things are coming, bad things will be happening. They already are, to a degree, but G-d's goodness is still abounding throughout the world, although not necessarily where we presume it to be found. I would urge everyone reading this book to not stand on the traditional teaching of comfortable religion "blessed by materialism," nor place their faith in the research and development of man.

    Only those standing on the Word of G-d will have the discernment to recognize the significance of world events as they continue to unfold. Scripture indicates that many of G-d's people will be alive at the time several of these calamities take place. The Revelation given to John, clearly revealed that many of G-d's people will face persecution, even death. But if the culmination of these last days occur in our lifetime, would there be a better way to be ushered into His presence and stand before His throne?

    The words of this book may sound dissenting, but they are the words of warning and of concern for our children's children. We cannot leave them the legacy of "fearful heresy" when G-d has given us the Good News. We cannot leave them to trust the world powers, when Y'hshuwah stated, "He has overcome the world."

    I am not anti-American, but as an American, I can see what is happening here. According to Scripture, the entire world is headed down the path away from G-d. I don't believe in replacement theology, but I do believe the passage that I have quoted extensively throughout this book, "there is nothing new under the sun." The sons of Ishmael continue to war, even amongst themselves, as

Scripture stated they would. From the headlines, it can be gleaned, the only thing that seems to truly unite the Arab nations is their jealous hatred of Israel and their disgust of American materialism. Israel, as a newly re-established nation, continues to make the same mistakes as recorded in Scripture. America has made every mistake ancient Israel ever did and exerted all the authority that Pharaoh, Nebuchadnezzar, and Caesar ever claimed.

As a world "super power" or a nation clinging to that status, we are leading the way into Technocracy. We either establish the standard or attempt to hold other nations accountable with our technology, or we sell it as consumer goods. As I am writing this statement, 20 billion dollars worth of weapons have just been promised to our oil supplying "ally." I could truly elaborate a different direction right here, in that fifteen of the nineteen terrorists of 9/11, had passports from Saudi Arabia. I don't know why we consider that nation to be our ally, and I certainly can't understand why we've chosen to make a 20 billion dollar weapon's deal with them. That being said, getting back to the topic at hand, our technology is valuable around the world, because the entire world values and places a great deal of hope in technology, often American technology. There are a myriad of examples in which we have placed our trust in technology, and if not technology, in America, itself.

In many areas, we still tend to think of technology as large and looming and distantly advanced or optionally avoidable, but it's quite close and personally affects most of us in this country and many others. Obviously, anyone with a home computer is aware of the possibilities with technology, but those who have not yet made that leap are still dependent upon technology in many personal ways. The fear around Y2K taught us that we already have a dependency upon technology and a glitch of any magnitude would affect nearly every part of our lives. We see technology at the local store as our items are scanned at check out. We see technology in the sound system at the local church or synagogue. And of course, we see technology in every part of our mobile society from I-pods and cell phones to traffic lights and the cameras sitting above them.

As we see technology on the large scale, there is also a branch of technology that is incorporating itself into individual lives by choice. Technology has now made it possible to identify individuals through biometrics and DNA, which is another acronym that I used throughout the book. I used it merely on presumptuous recognition, as it's been a part of scientific awareness, even to laymen, for some time. DNA stands for deoxyribonucleic acid, the basic cellular component for genetic and hereditary identity. This has become such a "comfortable" acronym that people don't even look beyond the potential ramifications any more. The majority of the world willingly submits to DNA sampling in attempts to either prove identity or prove ancestry. Some of the reasons and hope to attain acclaim through submission of DNA, are truly sad. In the attempt to prove themselves related to somebody, they apparently never consider that their most personal information is being included in a universal data bank.

There is no doubt in my mind, DNA data bases will at some point serve to coordinate the contents of the genetic information of millions even billions; making it available to government, medicine, law enforcement, and who knows . . ., through centralized communication.

Neither give heed to fables and endless genealogies, which minister questions, rather than G-dly edifying which is in faith: so do.   *I Timothy 1: 4*

Technology is keeping many little places on the globe pretty comfortable and efficient, and affording most of the big places on the globe greater expansion and authority. We can clearly see that governments around the world are changing. In following headlines, it would appear that most are changing to gain control and power, while still attempting some sort of cohesive cooperation with other governments.

America is home to Henry Ford, the Wright Brothers and Bill Gates. Technological advancement is not necessarily a bad thing, but when it's blatantly leading to the fulfillment of prophesy against G-d, it becomes a horrible thing. Just as in the case of Adam and Eve, the blame does not lie exclusively with the innovation, because each of us makes a definitive choice.

I'm going to give a brief outline, not a timeline, per se, but a method of arrival, as we move further toward technological dependency. Plutocracy is a system of politics in which the wealthy make governing decisions, and can certainly be a part of any republic or democracy. Plutocracy is the power that funds the emergence of technocracy from a republic or a democracy. Anticipatory Democracy is the line between voluntary participation and mandatory involvement. Anticipatory democracy is not a free democracy, but rather the transitional step between a constitutional republic or democracy, to be managed by the rule of law.

Anticipatory Democracy is political jargon for legislating required participation, to specified standards. Ecology has become green politics and seems to be the most prominent and outstanding example of Anticipatory Democracy, at this time. Care for our planet and ecology is being lead by the experts, doctors and scientists, and promoted by the politicians. These scientists claim the same authority over the condition of our planet that physicians do regarding the health of the human body. As more laws are enacted to save the planet, the rights of the people will be exchanged. For the majority of humanity, scientists are already making health decisions, it will just expand to the health of the planet as well, in this end time technocracy. Science is predicting the end of the world by global warming. They say the earth will be consumed by the heat of the sun. That information was already included in G-d's Word nearly 2000 years ago, in the 16th chapter of the Revelation. Buying into all the green solutions, in an attempt to prohibit the fulfillment of prophecy will not resolved this issue. Attempting to eliminate a carbon footprint will simply result in leaving a trail of fool's gold.

Some energy companies have the capability and are seeking the power to control the temperature in new homes and businesses from the corporate office with the flick of a switch to prevent energy waste. While many Energy companies are actually encouraging their customers to lobby their representatives to reduce costs, or so we are told. Clearly this is not the chosen method of Exxon.

Anticipatory Democracy comes about without any new election or amendment, or with a majority desiring and willing to work for great change. I can't speak for other countries, but usually in this one, with change there is a mantle of power that is given to those that are considered the most skilled and knowledgeable in the endeavor. This action simply shifts the power from one leader to another, and away from the common people, a.k.a. citizens. Semantics and redefinition are keeping the appearance of this transition, for the time being, to be subtle. The segues for connecting the powers are already in place, and easily identifiable in our society.

The Washington lobby connects science and

technology with the government, commerce, and the consumer, sometimes referred to as the constituent, and will insist we all participate.

Insurance connects health care with the government, commerce, databases, and the consumer, no longer referred to as patient.

Certainly the military has promised large dividends both in education and finances, which connects many of the end time powers with the government and the soldier, that is the citizen in service.

Books, tapes, and music, have connected religion with entertainment, education, commerce, and the consumer, and in the case of a 501c3, the government.

Entertainment connects the media with politics, commerce, and the consumer, who frequently refer to themselves as informed listeners, and entertainment drowns out the voice of G-d.

Politicians, pundits and preachers will bring it all together with tax exempt donations, special memberships, and tithes.

We know Islam places their holy book above all else. I am not saying their book is holy, but simply that they count it to be holy and the standard for their decisions. Their religious beliefs shape their politics and policies. And we know many of Israel's political decisions are based upon Talmud and the traditional teachings of the sages.

In America, however; many writings and teachings are more influential than Scripture. A quasi religious, politically correct, scientific, materialistic society has already crossed the Threshold of Technocracy. The book of Acts referred to the writings found in the Greek democracy as "curious arts." Here are the various references that have been interwoven and accepted in our culture and considered to be complimentary to Scripture, or at least not viewed in opposition.

The following list of ten books, concepts, and ideologies have become completely intertwined in our American Judeo-Christian culture, all the while claiming, a separation of religion and government, in the powerful tradition of Rome.

Here is the list that I call

the TEN COMPROMISES

1. The Big Book of AA - Higher Power, yet self defined . . . gods of our own understanding - self. Anyone who thinks they can define, or understand their god, is their god. AA claims to be a spiritual program, without a church or synagogue or even a specific god, other than an unopened bottle. Of course AA is not the only organization redefining spirituality. There are people who refer to themselves as very spiritual and call themselves pagans. There are also many that combine secular concepts with Biblical teachings, such as motivational speakers and Christian psychologists.

2. The Constitution is an exquisite document for a government, and I'm glad America has the one we have, but it is not to be revered, worshiped or held on the same plane as Scripture. The Constitution does not prove us to be a G-dly nation. The Constitution was written and designed to protect our sovereignty as a nation and from fundamental changes in government with change in leadership. The Bill of Rights is a wonderful list of important facets of life, but G-d is truly the one that gives us our freedoms and our protection. Neither of these pieces of paper, regardless of their earthly value and time honored importance to this nation, are equivalent with Scripture.

3. The PDR and Merck Manual gives names, labels, and specifics of pharmaceuticals. PDR is an acronym for Physician's Desk Reference, so some of the information contained is beyond the knowledge of the general public. This large book is the guiding reference for physicians writing prescriptions and pharmacists filling them. Every drug that has met FDA approval is listed. The Merck Manual helps the layman self-diagnose. Both books are common place in America.

4. Personal Interpretation of the New Testament or Torah allows working and shopping on Sabbath and Sunday. Personal interpretation, for many, has become as revered as the Word of G-d, Itself, and overridden the example set by Messiah. Personal interpretation has allowed Materialism to take root and grow beyond what anyone could have imagined. Yet, never do we consider our material excess to be idolatry, or to quote Genesis "household gods."

5. Dr. Spock, Dr. Phil, Dr. Dobson. Every school of thought offers a doctor to tell us how to raise our children. We hear the concept promoted that "Knowledge is Power." I believe Eve also heard something to that effect in Genesis 3: 5. Education is not wisdom, money isn't happiness and clearly power does not bring peace.

Parents are no longer raising children because there are many single parent homes and in many cases if there are two parents in the home, they both work. Children grow up hearing money discussed at home, quite frequently. Whether parents think so or not, it's true. Children are programmed very early to see the progression; more education > more money, more money > more power, more power > more of everything, the way I want it. Children are literally growing up in an institutionalized setting to be cared for and unfortunately medicated to be grouped when they are of the age to still be one on one, with mom. So, since we are no longer raising children according to Scripture, more books are written to explain how it should be done in our society.

6. America has selective beliefs of the Old Testament, usually in regard to war and punishment, and a primary disregard of many of G-d's statutes. We've somehow gotten the idea, the Old Testament is available for perusal and when it suits our purpose, it is to be quoted and used. There is no place in the New Testament that tells G-d's people to declare war. Actually Y'hshuwah said, "don't even use defense tactics." There is no place in the New Testament that commands we are to exact punishment, corporal or capital. When barbarism is legislated into "civilized society," it's not heathenistic, if "we" do it. What is wrong for an individual is still unethical en masse.

A nation that lives by military might and law enforcement is always going to be under constant threat of attack. Living under constant threat of attack yields fear, heart problems, and an aggressive society.

7. Laws on the books. It's truly amazing how many people devoutly believe that laws protect their freedom, until it comes to the things of G-d. Calling G-d's laws, religious legalism, while making our own laws, is idolatry. We know every society must have rules and laws and record transactions to exist as a society. We must have deeds and marriages and business transactions recorded to maintain our civilization, but we needn't have eliminated G-d when we legislated order. Legislating new laws while ignoring G-d's ordained statutes has caused us to need more laws in an attempt to maintain order. The

Old Testament doesn't contain nearly the number of laws as are on the books in our nation's capitol. The Old Testament doesn't contain half the number of ordinances we are burdened with on a local level.

When man defines "right," he's met G-d's definition of "wrong." Living by laws other than G-d's, while claiming to be G-dly, is referred to in Scripture as spiritual adultery, in the prophets. There are four initials that I've seen on everything from bracelets to bumper stickers: WWJD? It's a widely recognized acronym that stands for What Would Jesus Do? When it comes to the laws of G-d, do we really have to ask what he would do?

8. The DSM is the bible for those who will ultimately be in control of the captivity of many . . . Health and incarceration have been brought together by HIPAA and mental health initiatives to either protect us from dangerous people or defective people from themselves. DSM and HIPAA are two more acronyms that weren't included in the chapter that addressed acronyms. HIPAA is Health Insurance Portability and Accountability Act. I've been privy to sit in on the explanation when it was first introduced, supposedly to protect a patient's privacy and assure the best possible care.

In the current explanation, the patient is now the consumer. The Diagnostic and Statistical Manual is the bible of mental health professionals. I mentioned in a previous chapter, just a couple of the diagnoses the professionals make through the labeling assigned in this ever expanding and evolving handbook. The DSM is numbered, (in Roman numerals, I might add), indicating the revisions that take place as diagnoses are added or deleted and labels expanded. The fourth revision is presently the authority used by the practitioners. Between the DSM-IV and Talk Radio, it won't be long until free thinking is completely in the past tense, replaced with programming and/or medication.

In a previous chapter, I mentioned being a visitor in a hospital and told I could "use the phone." Thanks to HIPAA, when they don't let us use the phone, no one will be able to find out what happened to us . . .

9. People, Enquirer, media, church, and talk radio: Revised dictionary and revisionist's history. Filtered information is not honest information. Most talk radio hosts say they are not reporters, they are entertainers. And speaking of entertainers, pundits are not the only entertainers that are mistaken to be providing information for life. Preachers have become pretty entertaining in their own right, at least those with a sizeable following have. Where the pundits can rouse an audience through judgment and condemnation of political differences, many modern preachers are choosing to rally their listening audience, one of two ways. Although a few can balance both, the religious groups are predominantly divided between fighting the good fight against social immorality or the promise of prosperity.

The idea of taking a "good philosophy" and connect it to a couple of 1/2 Scriptures in or out of context is absolutely not going to sustain anyone through the times that are ahead, much less bring them to a genuine relationship with G-d; but it is popular. I've mentioned more than once, the complete incongruence between psychology and Scripture.

Christian Psychology has become the "tongues" of the modern religious day and Prosperity the sign of G-d's blessing and approval. I think an equation, best explains my point.

Pseudo-science + Religious rhetoric =
Corporate Christianity

Translation: Big Book Sales

. . . and big book sales means recognition, which can lead to fame and importance, which ultimately means huge political influence, which means prosperity, and that, "they" tell us, is the sign of G-d's approval.

The Christians will probably never catch up with the deceased Rebbe Schneerson, in their influence in Washington, but the evangelicals en masse are a power at the polls. We've seen this very issue, throughout the '08 presidential primaries, with endorsements, rejections, and a few changes of absolve between the politicians, the pundits and the preachers.

Rather than seeing the lame walk, blind eyes opened, and the dead raised, there's plenty of empty talk, wallets opened, and buildings raised.

Paul referred to this particular method of preaching as "tickling itching ears."

For the time will come when they will not endure sound doctrine; but after their own lusts shall they heap to themselves teachers, having itching ears;

II Timothy 4: 3

The world does not need religious gatherings that encourage us to feel better in our big mess, or more religious politics. We need to get back to the truth of Scripture that G-d is bigger than our mess, but HE still calls our mess, SIN. And many of the things that we have given ourselves permission to do, HE still calls sin. Sin not only needs G-d's forgiveness; but to receive His forgiveness, G-d requires our repentance!

Repentance is the change and Y'hshuwah is the way, PERIOD. It is not negotiable, but it is simple, once self has been dethroned.

While today's trendy teachings, both religious and secular, are permeating the emotions of the average

247

listener, the average listener is not having their soul fed by the truth of the Living G-d.

10. Wish lists have become abundant, from catalogues to e-bay. Is it good for me? I need what they have. This is America, land of welfare opportunity, disability advocacy, and amnesty, if . . . one is willing to be owned. Equal opportunity has come to mean entitlement. "I paid into it," means the old math really taught no concept of understanding percentages. Our present economic circumstance is only a foretaste of what's to come through these last days. Our days of power and prosperity at our own command were truly not short lived, but they are coming to a close. We can look around and see the waste, and yet the insatiableness at the same time.

I've literally seen people that neglect their own possessions and properties in attempting to gain the possessions and properties of others. The world is full, and certainly America is not the exception, here, of people who don't want what they have, but they don't want someone else to have it, and they always want something more. Our covetous nature as human beings often convinces us of a horrible deception, a strong delusion. The more we want, the more we should have, and the more we should obtain, then the more that must be protected, and the more someone else can take away. Ultimately creating a cycle that connects our values to our material possessions and our material possessions are deeply connected to money.

So is he that layeth up treasure for himself, and is not rich toward G-d.   Luke 12: 21

Y'hshuwah called money, mammon. But here in America, we call it prosperity and blessing. In other countries excessive greed by the ruler or ruling class, depending upon the leader, is called tyranny, fascism, totalitarianism, or a dictatorship. Regardless of the euphemism, labels or judgment, it is mammon that formulates the bond, either alliance or opposition, and sets the standard for humanity in the 21st Century.

While cultures around the world are being told to fear everything and being convinced to hate other ideologies, there is a silent war looming, actually already defeating many. Economic warfare is being won without firing a shot, and economic warfare will bring down a materialistic society that has no standard for it's currency.

There is a government looming on the horizon that will ultimately insist that it's constituents, (subjects) believe and state "And my government shall supply all my . . ." Most would say they would never state such a thing, and certainly would never believe that. Regardless of what they say they believe, many are already living that lifestyle.

While we are being promised fearful safety and unending global vigilance, we've missed the fact that this ideology translates to nothing more than anxiety and captivity. The backdoor to despotism is to label questioning, dissidence; and to reward silent submission. Religious nationalism is building while the world ignores G-d's warning and invitation, yet, He continues to patiently offer both.

. . . When I say unto the wicked, Thou shalt surely die; and thou givest him not warning, nor speakest to warn the wicked from his wicked way, to save his life; the same wicked man shall die in his iniquity; but his blood will I require at thine hand. Yet if thou warn the wicked, and he turn not from his wickedness, nor from his wicked way, he shall die in his iniquity; but thou hast delivered thy soul. Again, When a righteous man

doth turn from his righteousness, and commit iniquity, and I lay a stumbling block before him, he shall die: because thou hast not given him warning, he shall die in his sin, and his righteousness which he hath done shall not be remembered; but his blood will I require at thine hand. Nevertheless if thou warn the righteous man, that the righteous sin not, and he doth not sin, he shall surely live, because he is warned; also thou hast delivered thy soul. And the hand of YHWH was there upon me; and he said unto me, Arise, go forth into the plain, and I will there talk with thee.
Ezekiel 3: 17b-21

When people get comfortably smug in their religious traditions, the society crumbles. The enemy is well aware of this fact. We can read example after example of ancient Israel in Scripture. It's obvious with the Pharisees in the New Testament. Rome clearly mandated civil law based upon religious or secular whim, and we can read headline after headline in America. I'm not, for one minute, insinuating that America is worse than the rest of the world, I am however; stating that nationalism and pride doesn't make us any better, and it certainly doesn't make us G-dly. With all of the failed examples in Scripture, we in America continue to attempt the legislation of morality or immorality by the elective choice of man. Y'hshuwah told John, very clearly, the description of the lifestyle of his people in the last days and the definition of saints.

Here is the patience of the saints: here are they that keep the commandments of G-d, and the faith of Y'hshuwah.   *Revelation 14: 12*

As the last days continue to unfold, we'll continue to see some religious influence in world governments and we'll see a great deal of governmental influence in religion.

At this juncture, any government or person, for that matter, that does bring workable solutions toward global unity is to be recognized for what Scripture states that entity is. False messiahs will offer solutions in a "form of godliness" but certainly at the hand and power of man.

Messiah will bring peace, lasting peace, and He is the only one that will, and He will bring it by the power of G-d. Just as John warned, though, false messiahs are already among us with some of the devastating results already visible. Every government and every leader that is striving for peace outside of Messiah's return, or endeavors to bring us to the brink of Armageddon is leading us one step closer to the beast of a one world government.

And the dragon was wroth with the woman, and went to make war with the remnant of her seed, which keep the commandments of G-d, and have the testimony of Y'hshuwah Messiah [Jesus Christ]. Revelation 12: 17

Regardless of whether the name of Messiah is in Hebrew or King's English, this passage clearly states G-d's people believe in Messiah and keep G-d's commandments.

Reality Check and Glorious Reassurance!

Through the world's problems known in prophecy as the Great Tribulation, just where will G-d's people be? According to I Thessalonians 4: 17, there is no time gap between believers being caught up and Messiah's return, which totally eliminates the concept of a pre-tribulation rapture. Scripture mentions three things specifically. G-d's people who are alive through the time of the Great Tribulation will be kept and provided for, bear His mark, or be martyred. For those believers that are still alive upon Messiah's return, and some will be, they will be caught up to meet him at his descent, and will ever be with him. The last days are indeed frightening and exhausting, but we have been given a choice with promise.

And YHWH shall be king over all the earth: in that day shall there be YHWH, and His name one.
Zechariah 14: 9

And he showed me a pure river of water of life, clear as crystal, proceeding out of the throne of G-d and of the Lamb. In the midst of the street of it, and on either side of the river, was there the tree of life, which bare twelve manner of fruits, and yielded her fruit every month: and the leaves of the tree were for the healing of the nations. And there shall be no more curse: but the throne of G-d and of the Lamb shall be in it; and His servants shall serve Him: And they shall see His face . . .
Revelation 22: 1-4

And he saith unto me, Seal not the sayings of the prophecy of this book: for the time is at hand.
Revelation 22: 10

Epilogue

Fear not, little flock; for it is your Father's good pleasure to give you the kingdom.

Luke 12: 32

www.ingramcontent.com/pod-product-compliance
Lightning Source LLC
Chambersburg PA
CBHW070852290526

45795CB00001B/83